AVAILABILITY:
Gabriel Marcel and the
Phenomenology of Human Openness

AMERICAN ACADEMY OF RELIGION
STUDIES IN RELIGION SERIES

edited by
Stephen Crites

Number 14
AVAILABILITY:
Gabriel Marcel and the
Phenomenology of Human Openness

by
Joe McCown

SCHOLARS PRESS
Missoula, Montana

AVAILABILITY:
Gabriel Marcel and the
Phenomenology of Human Openness

by
Joe McCown

Published by
SCHOLARS PRESS
for
The American Academy of Religion

Distributed by

SCHOLARS PRESS
Missoula, Montana 59806

AVAILABILITY:
Gabriel Marcel and the
Phenomenology of Human Openness

by

Joe McCown

Library of Congress Cataloging in Publication Data
McCown, Joe
   Availability : Gabriel Marcel and the
phenomenology of human openness.

   (Studies in religion series ; no. 14)
   Bibliography: p.
   1. Marcel, Gabriel, 1889-1973. 2. Self (Philosophy)
3. Phenomenology. I. Title. II. Series: American
Academy of Religion. AAR studies in religion ; no.
14.
B2430.M254M3   194   77-22358
ISBN 0-89130-144-5

Printed in the United States of America
1 2 3 4 5

CONTENTS

for Helen and Carroll–

whose remarkable openness as human beings I have,
only recently, begun to realize.

INTRODUCTION

Gabriel Marcel's writings pose special problems for interpretation. His interpreter is faced with the task of presenting a body of ideas, to which the author himself was never inclined to give the formality of a philosophical treatise. Marcel's original intention *was* to construct a systematic work. However, he realized early in his career that his own manner of reflecting was not suited to a style of writing which, since McLuhan, we have come to understand as linear: pursuing a line of reasoning which assumes certain first principles as clear and evident, and moving from these to the corollaries and conclusions which logically follow. Since 1925, Marcel has given up the ambition of writing a systematic work, and has instead been publishing his lectures as he had given them, and his journal notations as he had recorded them. When Marcel's friend, M. Roger Troisfontaines, came to him with an outline he had prepared as a stimulus for Marcel to give his writings an organized form, Marcel asked Troisfontaines, as a favor, to assume the task himself.[1]

In 1949, as he delivered the Gifford Lectures at the University of Aberdeen, Marcel looked back on his philosophical thought of over twenty years, and tried to show, not his system, but the *way* along which he had come.

> The image that imposes itself on me is that of a road. It is just, so it seems to me, as if I had been following what tracks there were across a country that appeared to me to be largely unexplored, and as if you had asked me to construct a main road in the place of those uninterrupted paths, or perhaps rather—but it comes to the same thing—to draw up a sort of itinerary.[2]

He noted in his journal that his thought appeared to him more and more like the process of finding his way.[3] This road or way (*via*) is one he has striven, in his reflections, not so much to lay out as to locate. And it is a way which is "narrow, difficult and perilous."[4] Or, as he describes it in other places, his way is circuitous and sinuous, characterized by windings and detours, determined by "the inevitably spiral character of that intellectual motion" which, he says, is one of the constants of his mind. This is not to say that Marcel frequently follows inconsequential tangents, or that his arguments cannot follow a straight line: a winding road may lead in a meaningful direction. But Marcel honestly admits, and does not disguise from his readers, the doubt, the anxiety and the mental gropings which are involved in each of his discoveries. "These gropings," he says, "are like the useless roundabout routes (*detours*) taken by a raw tourist in a country with which he has not made himself familiar."[5]

Marcel has said that the word "search" (*recherche*) ought to appear in every title to his philosophical writings. He originally intended to entitle his

1

Gifford Lectures, "A Search for the Essence of Spiritual Reality (*Recherche Sur l'Essence de La Réalité Spirituelle*)."[6] Marcel's term *recherche* is sometimes translated as research. "Research," in the academic sense, is probably the most misleading way to translate this word: something like quest, inquiry (as in a dialogue), investigation ("prospecting"), or simply "search" would better convey Marcel's intent.[7] He once said of the first part of his *Metaphysical Journal:*

> I was searching for no place in particular and I did not know whom I would meet or what I was about to discover. The very uncertainty of the situation drove me on and sustained me. I was like an explorer who sets out to trace a river to its original source. All I could say beforehand is that I was starting in a definite direction.[8]

Marcel, the philosophical wanderer (*homo viator*), is always, like Karl Jaspers, making "calls," or appeals, to other wanderers along his way, taking their sympathetic responses, when they come, as an indication that this is the way he should go. His philosophy makes an appeal, not to rational argumentation, but to experiences shared in common with his listener: a condition which is human, common bonds of feeling and location.[9]

Marcel's writings, while they do not exhibit a formal logic of argumentation, do contain a certain interior logic: a logic of coherence. All of Marcel's categories of analysis are intimately interconnected, and an understanding of any one of them will elucidate all the others. At the same time, an understanding of any of his categories requires at least an acquaintance with all the others. Every analysis he offers both enriches and implies every other. For instance, his phenomenology of hope takes on added depth and understanding, when read in the light of his descriptions of love and fidelity. In turn, the descriptions of love and fidelity are lacking in dimension when they do not include the descriptions of communion, mystery, presence, the thou. . . . The reader of Marcel should frequently return to what he has earlier read—and he should freely make cross-references from what Marcel has written at one point to what he has written at another. I hope that this interpretation of Marcel will be read in the same way. I have suggested in footnotes at various places references that could be made to other places of this book, as well as to other works by Marcel.

It is essential to my purpose that my reader discover for himself the coherence Marcel's philosophy exhibits. The central focus of this work is upon the concept of availability. On the level of an interior logic, I will try to show how Marcel's descriptions of availability are connected with his phenomenology of the lived body and with his investigations of such mysteries as presence, communion, hope, love, fidelity and the absolute Thou. Reflection upon the notion of availability involves us increasingly in the full scope of Marcel's philosophical adventure. On the level of ontological investigation, I hope to show how the intent of availability invites and invokes a participation in what Marcel calls the mystery of being. Availability engages us with being at different levels of intensity and intimacy: in the unreflected and bodily being of our incarnation; in the being in community to which our bodies present us, a being luminous with presence; in the being in the area of sacredness, where grace abounds and mystery is profound.

I am writing on Marcel from the perspective of the theologian. But I am not trying to seduce Marcel into any theological camp. In 1946, at the Congress of Rome, Marcel accepted the term "Christian Existentialist" as a description of his philosophical stance. The following year, he approved the title *Existentialisme Chrétien* for a collection of essays on this thought. However, he has since rejected this categorization of himself. He thinks the word "existentialism" is ugly, and besides too closely associated with the writings of Jean-Paul Sartre; and he wants to avoid the doctrinaire implications of an understanding of his work as a Christian or Catholic philosophy.[10] In an Author's Preface to the English Edition of the *Metaphysical Journal,* he relates that one of his students once asked him if his philosophy could not be considered as a kind of "neo-Socratism." He wonders whether this description would not be "the least inexact" that could be applied to him. "Neo-Socratism" would suggest the attitude of open inquiry which I have already mentioned as characteristic of Marcel's mind; it would also indicate Marcel's insistence on dialogue as essential to intellectual discovery and to communication.[11]

Without trying to "fit" Marcel into any theological or philosophical spectrum, I have tried to follow him in his exploration of the experiential grounds for the apprehension of mystery and holiness. For Marcel, those attitudes which are essential to a full and human life are the same attitudes which locate us in a religious view of our world: hopefulness, faith and, most fundamentally, availability. For availability describes human being inclined toward, disposed toward the sacred, and at the same time describes the way of human being to abounding, maturing life.

Marcel believes that a concrete philosophy of human experience is naturally attracted to the data of the Christian faith. He writes that

> for the christian, there is an essential agreement between christianity and human nature. Hence the more deeply one penetrates into human nature, the more one finds oneself situated on the axes of the great truths of christianity.[12]

This does not mean that the philosopher can infer the data of Christian revelation from an examination of the structures of authentic humanity. But it does mean that if you scratch deeply enough beneath the surface life of the authentic man, you will find the man of faith, the person open to the Presence and grace of the holy.

Paul Ricoeur writes that "the historical significance" of Marcel's thought is

> to repair the foundations for a possible theology, natural and supernatural—below the level of argument, at the level of feeling and attitudes which root thought at once in existence and being, in flesh and in Spirit—to restore "a certain living order in its integrity," in the being to whom a revealed word can be simply heard.[13]

The phenomenological analysis of availability functions in this sort of "foundational" way, preparing the grounds for a possible later reflection, opening thought for an acceptance of presence, illuminating what is fundamental to any faithful and hopeful participation in being. Pietro Prini writes of availability as "the central theme of the Marcellian methodology of metaphysical knowledge." He sees that

> Marcel has traced, with an extraordinary richness and variety of perspectives, the lyrical, logical and ethical conditions of our availability to the "unveiling" of Being in the world of existence. No one, in my opinion, can pose the same problem . . . [of ontological knowledge] without taking the same approach, even should he come to different conclusions.[14]

[1]Roger Troisfontaines, S.J., *De l'Existence à Être: La Philosphie de Gabriel Marcel,* I, Bibliotèque de la Faculté de Philosophie et Lettres de Namur (2d. ed.; Louvain: Éditions Nauwelaerts, 1968; Paris: Béatrice-Nauwelaerts, 1968), p. 376.

[2]Gabriel Marcel, *The Mystery of Being,* Vol. I: *Reflection and Mystery,* trans. by G. S. Fraser (5th ed.; Chicago: Henry Regnery Company, 1969), p. 4.

[3]Gabriel Marcel, *Presence and Immortality,* trans. by Michael A. Machado and rev. by Henry I. Koren (Pittsburgh: Duquesne University Press, 1967), p. 7.

[4]Gabriel Marcel, *Position et Approaches Concretes du Mystère Ontologique,* Philosophes Contemporains: Textes et Études (2d. ed.; Louvain: Éditions Nauwelaerts, 1967; Paris: Béatrice-Nauwelaerts, 1967), p. 88.

[5]Gabriel Marcel, *Le Mystère de l'Être,* Vol. I: *Réflexion et Mystère* (Paris: Aubier, Éditions Montaigne, 1951), p. 13. Cf. Gabriel Marcel, *Du Refus à l'Invocation* (Paris: Gallimard, 1940), p. 53. And cf. Gabriel Marcel, *Homo Viator: Introduction to a Metaphysic of Hope,* trans. by Emma Craufurd, Harper Torchbooks (3d. ed.; New York: Harper and Row, Publishers, 1965), p. 60. And Gabriel Marcel, *Philosophical Fragments (1909-1914) and the Philosopher and Peace,* trans. by Viola Herms Drath (Notre Dame, Indiana: University of Notre Dame Press, 1965), p. 127. Translations from the French are the author's own.

[6]Gabriel Marcel, *Searchings,* ed. by Wolfgang Ruf (New York: Newman Press, 1967), p. 94. And *Réflexion et Mystère,* p. 8. And cf. *Reflection and Mystery,* p. 2.

[7]*Réflexion et Mystère,* pp. 8, 15 and 213. And Gabriel Marcel, *Journal Métaphysique,* Bibliothèque des Idees (11th ed.; Paris: Librairie Gallimard, 1935), p. 155.

[8]*Searchings,* p. 94. Marcel may intend the word *recherche* to be a pun of sorts. He seems always to be uncommonly sensitive to the suggestiveness of language, and to the symbolic possibility for words to play on several registers.

[9]*Reflection and Mystery,* p. 262. Gabriel Marcel, *Being and Having: an Existentialist Diary,* trans. by Katharine Farrer, Harper Torchbooks (New York: Harper & Row, Publishers, 1965), pp. 199-200. Gabriel Marcel, *Metaphysical Journal,* trans. by Bernard Wall (Chicago: Henry Regnery Company, 1952), p. xii. *Presence and Immortality,* p. 26. *Position et Approches,* p. 88.

[10]See Roger Troisfontaines, *What is Existentialism?* Overview Studies (Albany, N.Y.: Magi Books, 1968), pp. 9-10.

[11]*Journal,* p. xiii.

[12]Gabriel Marcel, *Creative Fidelity,* trans. by Robert Rosthal (New York: Noonday Press of Farrar, Straus and Company, 1964), p. 79.

[13]Paul Ricoeur, *Gabriel Marcel et Karl Jaspers: Philosophie du Mystère et Philosophie du Paradox,* Artistes et Écrivains du Temps Présent (Paris: Éditions du Temps Présent, 1947), p. 276.

[14]Pietro Prini, *Gabriel Marcel et la Méthodologie de l'Inverifiable* (Paris: Desclée de Brouwer, 1953), pp. 119-120.

CHAPTER ONE
The Attitude of Availability

I. *Disponibilité:* Language and Attitude

The phenomenon Marcel locates and describes as availability discloses a surplus of meaning beyond the ordinary sense of the French word *disponibilité.* The meaning I am attempting to discover in availability—an "intent" which involves us in the social and sacral dimensions of our life—requires a distinction between a language and what I am calling an "attitude" of availability. Availability, from the nature of the phenomenon, seems to demand to be understood as an attitude. I mean this word in its basic sense as a position, a stance. The notion clearly has a bodily signification, referring to a direction we take, a way we face, or even more graphically, to a way in which our face is turned. Buber's word *Hinwendung* expresses well the basic "turn" of availability, and its bodily basis as well. Availability is a turn towards. . . . Marcel writes:

> It is essential to human life not only (what is obvious enough) to orientate itself towards something other than itself, but also to be inwardly conjoined and adapted—rather as the joints of the skeleton are conjoined and adapted to the other bones—to that reality transcending the individual life which gives the individual life its point, and, in a certain sense, even its justification.[1]

The significance of Marcel's notion of availability cannot be fully understood in the narrower sense of a formal philosophical concept. It cannot be understood only by referring to those few places in Marcel's writings where the term *disponibilité* occurs. The phenomenon of availability transcends its language. In this first section, I will try to show how Marcel's language of *disponibilité* allows, even requires, a surpassing of itself in the direction of a fuller sense of availability which I am indicating by the word "attitude." An attention to the ways Marcel uses the language of *disponibilité* will show why this is so.

Disponibilité is a word which cannot be adequately translated into another language. There is no one word, for example, in the English language which conveys everything Marcel suggests in his use of the term. Katharine Farrer, the translator of *Being and Having,* renders it "disposability," and in its negative form "non-disposability."[2] In his Gifford Lectures, given at the University of Aberdeen in 1949 and 1950, Marcel spoke of the difficulty of finding an "idiomatic English equivalent" for *disponibilité.*

7

At least neither I, nor the English translator of my previous work, *Being and Having,* managed to do so. The French terms I use are *disponibilité* and *indisponibilité.* Literally, in English, one would have to render these as availability and unavailability, but it might sound more natural if one spoke of handiness and unhandiness, the basic idea being that of having or not having, in a given contingency, one's resources to hand or at hand.[3]

Robert Rosthal, who translated *Du Refus á l'Invocation* (*Creative Fidelity* in the English), uses Katharine Farrer's word "disposability" in the text, but in a footnote suggests other English expressions: openness to the other, readiness to respond, forthrightness, as well as availability or spiritual availability.[4] Emma Craufurd, the English translator of *Homo Viator,* prefers "availability" to "disposability," but finds the phrase "at the disposal of" essential to translate the expression *á la disposition.*[5] Language difficulties which surround the concept of availability are not, however, cleared up when we have found a suitable word to translate *disponibilité.* For the more profound difficulty which appears here is that the term *disponibilité* is itself inadequate to convey the attitude Marcel has in mind.

The *Journal Métaphysique* presents in a special way the necessity of a distinction between a language and an attitude of availability. In this his first philosophical publication Marcel never used the word *disponibilité.* However, he did use words formed on the same root, in contexts in which he obviously is unconcerned with the attitude of availability. In a notation in the Journal dated February 22, 1919, the word *disponible* appears—a word Marcel uses to speak of the available person. In this context, however, Marcel is speaking of elements of our past we cannot "dispose of" forever (*non perpetuellement disponible*).[6] On February 25th, of that same year, he writes: "For a long time, in accord with Bradley, I had been disposed (*disposé*) to deny even that, that is to say, the absence of communication between the idea and its object."[7] And on March 3, 1919, in the context of a discussion of communication, he uses the expression *à sa disposition:* "Undoubtedly, the reason I can function as a source of information is that I am a definite someone, a him, who has a history, a certain collection of experiences at his disposal (*à sa disposition*)."[8] It is clear that Marcel does not intend an analysis of availability in any of these contexts.

Although Marcel never uses the word *disponibilité* in the Journal, he does give analyses which illuminate the *attitude* of availability. For example, it is here that Marcel first introduces the metaphor of "opening a line of credit to . . . ," which is the root metaphor for the attitude of availability. On February 2, 1922, he records some observations on community, intimacy and the possibility of a thou becoming for us "only a thou." We can mistake the measure of the intimacy we have achieved with another being. The trust or faith we place in another can always be betrayed—but only, according to Marcel, to the extent the thou remains a *him,* and we hold onto the possibility that one day we may have to say: "That miserable . . . ! *he* deceived me, *he* abused my confidence."

The possibility of doubt, and I would say, of denial sometime in the future is directly linked to the ambiguity in a relation of this sort. Let us imagine, on the other hand, that this ambiguity disappears, that the thou is no longer anything but a thou: to the extent this happens, doubt and denial become impossible, credit is no longer accorded with reservations about verification, it is opened without conditions.[9]

In *Être et Avoir*, Marcel notes that the notion of unavailability always implies that of transferable assets. (*Il me semble qu'elle implique toujours celle d'aliénation.*) To have unavailable capital always means to have capital which is partially depleted. (*Avoir des capitaux indisponibles, c'est les avoir partiellement aliénés.*) This is perfectly clear in the case of material goods. But Marcel wants to extend the notion to the case of sympathy. I am exposed to some misfortune which solicits my sympathy, but I cannot give it. I recognize that what "they" are telling me deserves, at least, my pity; still I feel nothing. "This is a strange thing. I want to experience this emotion which seems to *impose* itself on me. . . . but I feel nothing; I am not at my own disposal. (*Je ne puis disposer de moi-même.*)"[10]

In *Du Refus à l'Invocation*, Marcel again brings up the metaphor of credit, or "extending credit to. . . ." In this context, he makes it clear that he wants to relieve the metaphor of its material weight.

We must not be misled by the fact that to agree to extend credit is to place at the disposal [*à la disposition*] of another a certain sum, a certain quantity of something, with the expectation that it will be returned to us together with an additional sum, a certain profit. We must unburden the meaning of extending credit of this material weight.[11]

In *Foi et Réalité*, the second volume of *Le Mystère de l'Être*, Marcel shows how he means to do this. Freed of its material weight, the idea of "opening a line of credit" means: "I put myself at the disposal of, or again I make a fundamental engagement which bears not only on *what I have, but on what I am*."[12] We can in no way separate *ourselves* from what we offer to someone else. When we give credit to another, we are making a gift of ourselves. Too, we can only open a line of credit to someone, and never even to someone who "can be reduced to the condition which is that of things." Opening credit to . . . implies a placing of confidence in. . . . "I am sure that you (*tu*) will not betray my expectation; that you will respond to it, that you will fulfill it." We can only have confidence in some other who is a thou, a presence capable of being invoked, and of "being a recourse."[13]

Marcel's term *disponibilité* runs into particularly awkward difficulties with the phrase *disposer de*. For the attitude of availability is dispositionally opposed to an attitude which seeks "to dispose of" persons and things, and of persons as things; and the attitudinal opposition stands, although the term *disponibilité* is linguistically close to the infinitive, *disposer de*. "To dispose of" is to exercise a power, a power over a having. We can dispose of only what we have a power over, of whatever we *have* at our disposal: methods, instruments, information, categories. . . . We cannot dispose of a person, unless we consider the person as an instrument which we employ, or look at *him* as a possible source of information we would like to have. We can never dispose of *presence;* if we treat persons as things over which we have a power of disposal, they will invariably withhold their presence from us. This is as true in the case of persons who play at sex, as if it were a game, as in the case of the black maid who moves as a "non-person" through the household of a white family. Availability is an opening upon the presence of another, not a way of access to certain goods he possesses. Marcel writes that the available person is capable of being entirely with me; the unavailable person only gives me a provisionary loan on resources which lie at his disposal (*sur l'ensemble des ressources dont il est en mesure de disposer*).[14]

"To dispose of" has its fullest meaning, when we think of things we throw on a trash heap (and have trouble disposing of!). Perhaps, we can imagine that persons who have never "counted" (existed) for us can be "got rid of." But if a person does count in our lives, we think that he will continue to do so. "Disposing of" loses practically all its meaning in this case. We have to think of the life of the body as alien or strange to us, before we can "get rid of" living bodies. In time of war, we give The Enemy a name (such as "gook"), which sounds inhuman, and has the psychological value of preparing us for the business of war: getting rid of bodies.[15]

We can treat our own bodies as things at our disposal, only if we first estrange the life of the body from ourselves. The gnostic or the schizophrenic typifies this attitude. But the ultimate exercise of the power of disposal over our own bodies is suicide. Suicide is the limit case of an attitude which may already be the *moral* equivalent of suicide (or murder). Suicide is also the radicalization of unavailability. Marcel asks: "Doesn't someone who kills himself dispose of (*disposer de*) his body (or of his life), as if it were a thing? The lived body is a presence, at the disposal both of myself and others. The body suicide disposes of becomes an object, estranged from life, belonging no longer either to the self or the other." Someone who commits suicide "renders himself unavailable (*indisponible*) for others, or at least he acts like someone who, in a final sense, doesn't seem to care to remain available to them." On the other hand, "the being who is absolutely available (*disponible*) for others does not recognize the right to dispose (*disposer de*) freely of himself."[16] The attitude of availability should be distinguished from this "disposability" which is a power over a having.

Availability, as attitude, should also be distinguished from a sense of vacancy which the word *disponibilité* can suggest. In its military usage, *être en disponibilité* means "to be unattached" or "to be on half-pay." The attitude of availability does not signify an emptiness, as when the French speak of a *local disponible* (premises which are available).

> It designates, rather, an aptitude for giving ourselves to whatever presents itself, and for binding ourselves through the gift; or again for transforming circumstances into occasions, let us say, even into "favors," to thus collaborate with our own destiny, conferring on it our own mark.[17]

II. Indices to Unavailability

The surplus of meaning of the attitude of availability should be sought in availability's significance for personal and interpersonal life. Some indications of this meaning are given in Marcel's reflections on several ways unavailability may manifest itself: in encumbrance, crispation, susceptibility and moral ego-centricity.

A. Encumbrance

"To be unavailable," Marcel wrote in 1933, "is to be in some manner, not only occupied, but encumbered (*encombré*) by the self." The phrase, "in some manner," in this quotation is important, because the manner of self-encumbrance is what is decisive, not the form it takes. There is no difference, from this point of view, in being occupied with health, or with fortune, or with interior perfection.[18]

Marcel considers the example of the person who thinks about nothing else but the functioning of his organs, or the fitness or form of his physique. This person misses worlds of life, because he has become encumbered by a fascination with himself; his mirror image has him "caught" and is holding him. "Everything shows us that a being lives less, or if you wish, in a more indigent way, the more he is encumbered (*encombré*) with himself, entangled (*empêtré*) in himself."[19]

In an insightful passage in *The Mystery of Being*, Marcel compares the life of encumbrance to a hand-written page of manuscript, covered all over with erasings, scribblings, alterations.

> That is only a simile, of course, but its concrete meaning is that a life, let us say my life has been cluttered up [*encombrée*] with various odd jobs I have had to do, and perhaps, too, with amusements that met only some secondary interest of mine, that now I am no longer able to make out what is the relative importance of any particular occupation of mine as compared with any of my other occupations. I say the relative, not the absolute, importance: I am speaking solely of the importance of an occupation for me, not for others, nor from some ideal standpoint—of its importance merely from my own point of view. What is very strange indeed in this case is that I can no longer get at my own point of view. Thus I may, for instance, impose on myself a set of very wearisome duties, without taking account of the fact that they are in some sense fictitious duties, and that I would be far more true to myself if I had the courage to set myself free from them.[20]

An encumbrance is always cumbersome. Life is continually making calls upon our availability. It can happen that a person finds himself in a state in which he cannot respond to calls. The physical imagery Marcel uses to describe this state is suggestive. It is as if the call or appeal had come up against some material obstacle. An encumbered person literally cannot make room in himself for another. He is physically and emotionally incapacitated for response by the load of self-concern he carries, this "weight which at critical moments becomes literally unsupportable." The free act in this case would be the liberating act, the one which would lighten the load on our shoulders which "seems destined to one day throw our faces against the ground."[21]

Things are encumbering, because they get in the way; they interpose themselves between the self's presence to itself, and between the self and the presence of another. It is this interposition of things that Marcel has in mind when he writes of having as an "index to a possible unavailability." "To possess is almost inevitably to be possessed." The things we have may "have" us. We seem to have a natural inclination to identify our being with a having, and in this way to reduce the categories of ontology to meaninglessness. The dead man is the man who no longer *has* anything. We make ourselves consubstantial with the things we own, and we think that their loss means *our* impoverishment. If I have four things and give away two of them, I only have two left: *I am therefore impoverished.* It is true that the gift of the self, or the gift of presence, implies impoverishment, only if we think of our lives according to the categories of the things we own.[22]

We render ourselves unavailable as soon as we treat our lives as a having, in some way measurable, which can be wasted, used up, exhausted.

> When I identify myself with a having of this sort, I find myself in the state of chronic anxiety of the man hanging over the abyss, who possesses nothing but a small sum of money, which he must make last for as long as possible, because when it is gone, he will have nothing. This anxiety is a care which is gnawing and paralyzing, which blocks up every *élan,* every generous initiative. What we must see, is that anxiety or care can be reabsorbed into a state of interior inertia from which the world is lived as stagnation, as putrescence, . . . death-in-life, death anticipated.[23]

B. Crispation

The weight of encumbrance renders us incapable of presence. We become, in Marcel's word, opaque. The image he uses is that of a material which blocks the passage of light from one space to another. A transparent material lets the light through freely. A translucent material lets the light through dimly. An opaque material blocks the passage of light. The person who is opaque has ceased to let his presence pass into the world. He no longer lives in the world, nor remains open for its in-fluences (influx) upon his life.[24] In Marcel's analysis, an interior opacity is a sealing off of experience (*huis clos:* closed doors), so that experience becomes fixated on the stale, and tensed against the entrance of the new. Fixation is a hardening of the categories through which we view the world, and as such, a form of pride. (The Hebrew Scriptures knew that "hardening of the heart" proceeded from the will, and so was a form of pride.) Various images appear, scattered through Marcel's writings, to describe this form of unavailability. He uses the French word *crispation* (the English word is the same) to describe a shriveling and contraction, which are consequent upon a withdrawal into the self. The guiding image of the process of crispation is that of the crustacean animal who secretes around himself a shell which hardens with time, locking the world out as it locks itself in. The shell hinders free movement; its effect is de-pressing—the heaviness of the shell presses the animal down to earth.[25] Marcel writes that, "A hold on being is only possible through a sudden opening effected through this shell (*carapace*) which encloses (*environne*) us, and which we ourselves have secreted."[26]

A person only realizes himself in the act in which he tends to incarnate (embody) himself: in a work (*oeuvre*), in an action, or in an entire life. But at the same time, it is essential to the development of person-ality that it not crystallize or congeal (*figer*) around any particular expression of the self.[27] A coagulation of the life of the whole self around any particular adherence or manifestation of the self always means loss of sensitivity and a general devaluation of life. "For nothing in the world would I miss my Tuesday game of bridge, or my weekly session of chamber music, etc. . . . Piles of inconsequentials on top of nothingness."[28]

"Das fixierte Erlebnis wird leblos"—the fixated experience becomes lifeless. Lending ourselves, obsessively, to one world, we miss many broad and wonderful worlds. Our existence becomes unavailable for fresh life. Our life degenerates into existence, and becomes heavy with the "weight of existence."[29]

> The power to grasp is above all a power to lend ourselves, that is to say, to let ourselves be grasped (the role of the Kairoi). Hardening [*durcissement*]. Locking up [*tétanisation*], which results in my no longer lending myself. It is because I no longer avail myself that I am no longer available for others.[30]

Marcel's analysis of the fanaticized consciousness illustrates one way in which crispation can set in upon a human life. Marcel locates the roots of fanaticism, not in confidence ("unbalanced certainty"), but in "a mistrust of one's self, a fear which one does not admit to one's self."[31] The fanatic is in no way open, either to us or to the modification of a position he has taken up. He has sealed himself off. It is difficult for us to be *present* with a fanatic, for the fanatic is someone who has a fixed idea or obsession which he is compelled to defend. He becomes our adversary, and "handles what he calls his ideas as offensive weapons." So the fanatic necessarily puts us on the defensive. We are obliged to find some "defensive armour" for ourselves: either we must meet his (usually verbal) violence with violence, or we must refuse the battle.[32] The fanatic always says: "I affirm this, *I* do, whatever anyone else says." His claim conceals a wish to "wipe out" anyone who would challenge or deny it. He thinks of his opponents in the most degrading images possible: as animals—"lubricious vipers" or "hyenas and jackals with typewriters"—or as material objects to be overturned or smashed.[33]

Fanaticism has the same paralyzing effect on the mind as does tetanus on the body. The fanaticized consciousness remains numb and unsympathetic to "everything to which its own compass needle does not respond." It is just as if a patient were to fail to respond when a doctor sticks his foot with pins, or shines a light in his eye. (Fanaticism is a "pathological" phenomenon.) The fanatic is satisfied to think what "one thinks," to say what "one says," and to believe what "everyone knows." His words are empty of meaning, mere notions other men have put into his head. Truth has become degraded, for him, into prejudice and opinion. He has closed off the channels which lead to experience.[34] The fanatic is the opposite of the man who has kept himself open to fresh scenes and novel times.

> A life which opens on heaven: but precisely the life of the pretentious bigot does not open on heaven. The latter is confused with the "country theatre" where everybody fights to get a front seat.[35]

C. Susceptibility

Susceptibility is an anguished unavailability. Marcel thinks it rooted in an anguish about the self, which is far from a legitimate love of the self. The susceptible person experiences his human vulnerability as unbearably painful—as an open wound.

> Encumbered [encombré] by myself, plunged into a disturbing world, which is sometimes menacing and sometimes my accomplice, I keep an anxious watch out for everything which might soothe or ulcerate this wound which I bear in myself, which is me [moi]. This state is strikingly analogous to that of someone who suffers from an abscessed tooth and tries to get relief, first with heat, then with cold, with acid, then with sugar.[36]

The anguish of susceptibility, according to Marcel, is the rendering experience of a basic contradiction: between a need to possess, to annex everything, thus creating a monopoly over all available goods; and an obscure consciousness of an abyss opening within the self, a consciousness that, in spite of every attempt to fill up the abyss, the self still is nothingness. The susceptible consciousness perceives itself as exposed to the twin ravages of time and criticism. "I can affirm nothing about myself which would be authentically me, my own self; there is no longer anything which could be permanent, nothing which could be sheltered against criticism and the duration of time." The susceptible person needs to be confirmed, from outside himself, by another. He craves esteem and possessions as protections against possible losses to which the passage of time renders him susceptible. And he wants desperately to *have* (or to have power over) the opinions of others, and to have things which will influence in his favor the regard (glances) of others. It is paradoxical that this most self-centered of persons needs the other: he waits upon the other, and upon him alone, for his final investiture.[37]

Marcel's description of the "shy young man" at a cocktail party illustrates the psychology of susceptibility. This young man feels highly self-conscious, and extremely, excessively vulnerable. He might be ignored, or wounded in a thousand different ways. It seems that everyone is looking at him, people he doesn't even know are looking at him. They must be making fun of his clothes, his tie must be crooked. He thinks that he is exposed to a "malevolent lucidity" in the glances of others. He is at once preoccupied with himself and hypnotized by others, paralyzed by what opinions he imagines "they" are forming of him.[38]

The susceptibility of self-consciousness is an unavailability, because the self-conscious imagination of what another is thinking about me throws up a sort of screen against the presence of the other. The susceptible consciousness projects its own feelings upon the other, and actually never reaches the other. The idea of the other—of his opinions and intentions—replaces the other. Marcel writes that one of the basic concepts of his work is that "self-consciousness, far from being an illuminating principle, as traditional philosophy has held, on the contrary shuts the human being in on himself and thus results in opacity rather than enlightment."[39]

D. Moral Ego-centricity

Marcel describes "moral ego-centricity" as the illusion "that I am possessed of unquestionable privileges which make me the center of my universe, while other people are mere obstructions to be removed or circumvented, or else those echoing amplifiers, whose purpose is to foster my self-complacency."[40] This illusion is "infinitely persistent," because it is constructed upon our most primordial experience of ourselves in the world. We all feel, naturally, that we are the center around which everything else gravitates, just as we feel that the sun and stars revolve about the earth.[41] Each one of us tends to construct around himself what Marcel calls an "ego-centric topography." We become the center of a lived time and space, arranged around ourselves in concentric zones of decreasing interest, concern, adherence. We feel space and time extending outward from our awareness of ourselves. Here is where we are, and now is our time; there and then lie at some distance from the central perspective which we occupy.[42]

These zones of decreasing adherence are also zones of increasing unavailability. We neither involve nor invest ourselves in what does not concern us. We are all unavailable in certain regions of our lives. The ego-centric topography which supports this unavailability is something more radical than self-love. Marcel wonders "if we could not define the whole spiritual life as the ensemble of activities through which we reduce in ourselves the part played by unavailability."[43]

He compares the egoist to the dreamer. Like the dreamer, the egoist moves along beyond the borders of reality, never actually crossing them. He reserves for himself the strange power of modifying situations without troubling himself about what effect his actions might have on those others who dwell in his world with him. He is beyond the reach of good, as well as evil. He has not yet awakened to reality.[44]

The experience of ourselves as the center of the universe is naive, in the sense that it is still untested by reality. While the unexamined life is centered on the self, the *human* life always finds its center outside itself. For Marcel, the notion of human life means a surpassing of the biological; human life includes but goes beyond the satisfaction of organic needs and instincts. A prisoner in jail, serving out a life sentence, eats and breathes, his body carries on the normal functions of biological life; but we would not hesitate to say that his existence is not life. Human life means also a reflected or examined life. From the human point of view, life can no longer be mere spontaneity. Reflection is "one of the ways in which life manifests itself," and "in a sense one of life's ways of rising from one level to another."[45]

The egoist lives a life which is less than human, because his life is unreflected—he has not mastered his own experience as experience in communication with other experiences. A full and concrete knowledge of ourselves cannot be, in Marcel's word, "heauto-centric"; paradoxically, it is always "hetero-centric."[46]

In other words, the conditions under which we become conscious of ourselves are essentially social. A sense of who we are always implicates some other person, either present or conceived, as a witness, a rival or an adversary. A child picks a bouquet of flowers and brings it to her mother. She holds out *herself* for admiration, as she holds out the bouquet. She calls upon a "you," her mother, for confirmation of herself. "It was I, I who am with you here, who picked these lovely flowers, don't go thinking it was Nanny or my sister; it was I and *no one else*." The adult, also, needs to be recognized in the sight of the other, although usually in a more subtle or sophisticated way. He hangs a painting, which he himself has done, on the wall of his living room. If someone asks him, "Who painted that? Van Gogh?" he will say, "No, as a matter of fact, I did." *Human* life is everywhere social, dialogical, communal. As Marcel says,

> the city which I form with myself . . . is not a monad . . . cannot establish itself as a distinct and isolated center, without working for its own destruction . . . on the contrary, it draws the elements of its life from what is brought to it along canals, often very badly marked out, from friendly cities, of which it often scarcely knows the name or the situation.[47]

Clarity about ourselves does not proceed from the direction of the ego, but from the direction of "the ego and its relation to others." Usually, when we are in the dark about ourselves, we will ask someone else—a friend, a psychiatrist—for illumination on ourselves. The ego, left to itself, is a cause of blindness. "It is because the egoist confines his thought to himself that he is fundamentally in the dark about himself. He does not know his real needs, he does not realize that he betrays himself just to the extent to which he concentrates all his attention upon himself."[48] The egoist acts as if he throws up barriers between himself and others, barring himself from their experience and their life: their understanding and love, their perspective upon his life (the perspective which might help him find the light and the way). The egoist is unavailable to himself, because he is unavailable to the other. He ends up knowing neither himself nor anybody else.[49] Marcel says that it is against such a condition that "the essential characteristic of the person is opposed, the characteristic, that is to say, of availability (*disponibilité*)."[50]

III. Indices to Availability

Marcel also discusses certain phenomena—self-presence, receptivity, welcoming—which indicate, in a more positive manner, the surplus (human) meaning of the attitude of availability.

A. Self-presence

Marcel notes in his metaphysical diary that the expression "self-presence" (*présence à soi-même*) is "misleading," but admits to himself that he is unable to find another more suitable word at the moment.[51] The notion of "a presence of the self to itself" (*une présence de soi-même à soi-même*) appears first in the *Journal Métaphysique*. Here Marcel observes that it should be conceived as "a certain interior link," never as a logical unity between two entities. He suggests that self-presence might be seen in the image of the soul married to itself, or in the image of "a certain interior city."[52] In *Homo Viator,* he attempts a definition of self-presence (*ma présence à moi-même*), as "the portion of creation which is in me, the gift which from all eternity has been given me of participating in the universal drama, of working, for example, to humanize the Earth, or on the contrary, to make it more uninhabitable."[53] Then he says that such definitions are bound always to be inadequate. Just as anyone who has loved knows that what he loves in another cannot be given in any definition—so the knowledge of who we are when we are ourselves (*present* to ourselves) is given to us only in love.[54]

There is, for Marcel, a convergence, even a coincidence, of self-presence with the presence of another. Self-presence (*la présence du moi à lui-même*) appears where the presence of the other is recognized.[55] Love is the paradigm of the revelation of self-presence, with the presence of the other. And availability is the attitude which permits this revelation. It is when we are open to ourselves that it is given to us to be open to others, available (*disponible*) for them. But it is just as true to say that when we are open to others we are most open to ourselves.[56]

> I can only communicate effectively with myself, when I communicate with the other, that is, when the other becomes thou [*toi*] for me. And this transformation comes about thanks to a movement of interior relaxation by which I put an end to a sort of contraction through which I shrivel [*crispe*] and at the same time distort [*déforme*] myself.[57]

In a context in which he is illustrating what he means by reflection, Marcel gives an excellent example of how availability for others moves into consonance with availability to ourselves, to the self we genuinely are, or can be. Consider a situation in which I have been deceived by the conduct of a friend of mine. It seems that, in the light of his action, I must revise my opinion of him: he is not the person I thought him to be. But then a memory flashes through my mind, a memory of something I once did. And I ask myself: "Was this act of mine really so different from the one I am now judging so severely? Am I, then, qualified to condemn someone else?" My question leads me to ask who I am and what I am worth. This reflection which I direct towards myself can create within me an anguished consciousness. However, if I carry my reflection far enough, the anguish may give way to a sense of liberation, which I experience as the overthrow of an obstruction. When I have overthrown the barrier my condemnation was forming, I am again available for my friend—and at the same time available to that region of myself which I have realized is liable to the same criticism I direct toward my friend.

> I have introduced the self which committed the act in question to the self which was not hesitating to judge; and I also—and this cannot be a simple coincidence—feel myself capable of entering more intimately into communication [*communication*] with my friend, now that there is no longer between us the barrier [*le barre*] which separated the judge from the accused man.[58]

This example shows, also, that self-presence is not invariably with us; it may be lost or eclipsed, and we are constantly having to rediscover it, to recover ourselves. There are certain moods of human being in which we find ourselves in a condition which Marcel describes as a feeling of being inwardly ruffled, or as a sense of the self as decentered, as alienated (*aliéné*).[59] Times of fatigue, of boredom, of sterility and aridity, of despair, can put us out of touch (the rupture of *communion,* in Marcel's language) with who we know we are, most of the time. Such attitudes, in which we are away from ourselves, seem always to make us indifferent to others. The presence of another always comes as a response to the gift of the self. When we have no self-presence to "present," we make ourselves unavailable to other presence.[60]

On the other hand, in moods in which we are "at ourselves," we can be available for others. Happiness, for example, is a mood we always want to share with others, a mood in which we want to share *ourselves.* In his Journal, Marcel asks himself if happiness is not one of the privileged moods in which we discover self-presence. (*Le bonheur ne serait-il pas une certaine façon d'être présent à soi-même?*)

> And [he continues] the more I am present to myself, the more others exist for me. This is the interior undividedness [*indivision*], which I spoke of in relation to the will, and which makes willing possible.[61]

B. Receiving and Welcoming

Marcel writes, in *Du Refus à l'Invocation,* that the positive aspect in availability is already given at the heart of receptivity. He then moves into an analysis of what it means to receive. (*Au vrai, qu'est-ce donc que recevoir?*) We should, he thinks, look at the fullest and richest meaning of receptivity. In its most impoverished form, to receive means to undergo. The empiricism of the eighteenth century spoke of "receiving an imprint," as a seal prints upon or "impresses" a mass of wax. In this case, to receive becomes synonymous with "to suffer"; it means "to submit passively to" (*subir*). Marcel sees a receiving of this sort as a limiting case. Descartes's piece of wax cannot function as the model for receptivity in its human forms. Marcel writes: "I hold, in principle, that we can speak of receiving (*reception*), and consequently of receptivity (*réceptivité*) only as a function of a certain readiness, a preparedness or a putting of our own house in order (*une certaine pré-affectation ou pré-ordination*)."[62]

The human meaning of receptivity obviously connects with the notion of self-presence. It is a receptivity which is welcoming (a reception). Human receptivity refers to a certain interior state, or attitude, which corresponds to, attunes itself to, an action upon the self. The model of this sort of receptivity is to receive, or to welcome (*accueillir*), a guest into a room or a home, or even into a garden. Persons do not receive on unknown terrain, as in a forest. We have to be "at home," as we receive—at home with ourselves or present to ourselves. The notion of a self (*un soi*) is definitely implied in human receptivity. *Someone* is needed who can reflect on himself as "me myself" (*moi*), who can say "I" and posit himself and be posited as an "I." Further, this self must experience as his particular domain an "area" (Marcel likes the English word) which is his own territory, a domesticated space. The self seems to be able to "impregnate" its surrounding world with its own qualities. This activity is what we commonly call "familiarizing" ourselves with our surroundings. When we "move into" a house or a neighborhood, we invest this zone of our in-habitation with our own intimacy. We begin to feel at home here; this becomes the place where we live. In such a place the distinction between our interior space and the space without us loses application. We lend *ourselves* to those places where we are at home; and such special places also come to reside within us. Consider, for example, the farmer who is torn away from the soil, or the sailor who is stranded in a strange port, separated from the sea. The feeling of being at home in certain "areas"—certain places and situations—is difficult to express in rational terms, so Marcel tries to *invoke* the experience he intends through recalling to us certain moods which are common to many: the distress of a child, when he is parted from his parents or his home, "the nameless sadness we have all experienced in certain hotel rooms."[63]

The human meaning of receptivity, then, is to introduce the other into a qualified (and privileged) zone of our experience or life, a region which is uniquely our own, which we have readied or prepared by investing something of ourselves in it. Receptivity—at least in this human sense of a reception—is not passive. At its center is an active element, something like a power of taking upon ourselves or into ourselves . . . (*comme le pouvoir d'assumer . . .*), or better still, the power of opening ourselves to . . . (*de s'ouvrir à . . .*). Reception transcends the dilemma of activity versus passivity: when the model of receptivity is located in human intercourse, it is no longer meaningful to speak in these terms.[64]

Marcel also speaks of the active aspect of our receptivity or reception as a gift, a gift of ourselves—or a sharing with another of "a certain reality, a certain fullness (*plénitude*)."[65]

Reception is also a *response* (here again, Marcel thinks that the English word is more revealing than the French *réponse*). His analysis of responsivity shows that response and appeal are linked together in one event, as are the active and passive moments of reception. A response is a reaction which comes from our interior depths (*cette réaction venue du tréfonds*). Marcel would like to reserve the word response for this wholly inward reaction which an appeal elicits. A reaction whose source is not within us, one which is forced upon us, is not a response. Someone who coerces our answer to his question or to his command forgets that we are men. In the measure in which we accede to his demand upon us, we cease to be present to ourselves; we become estranged from ourselves. An appeal is different from a demand in that we can refuse to give ourselves to it. And our *response* to an appeal is free, even liberating (it can take a load off our shoulders). A response to an appeal, "in a rather mysterious way," restores us to ourselves, at the same time as it co-responds to a situation outside ourselves, to the way in which others are affecting us.[66]

Marcel's analysis of reception as what is specific in the attitude of availability illuminates an otherwise vague notation he makes in his diary: that availability includes a certain "reference to . . ." or a "being in harmony with . . ." (*un être accordé avec . . .*). In Marcel's words, "the existential level" (*le niveau existentiel*) of availability differs from that of unavailability, and that difference coincides with the distinction between the open and the closed.[67]

The attitude of availability may be thought of according to the image of the open door. The openness of availability is positive; it indicates a concrete direction, towards the world and towards presence. Availability makes ready and makes room for otherness. It welcomes what is strange and novel, not necessarily adopting its strangeness, but admitting (in the sense of opening the door to) its presence. Perhaps, Marcel's best description of availability is his statement about the spirit of prayer: "The spirit of prayer, above all, is a welcoming (*accueillante*) disposition towards everything which can tear me away from myself, from my propensity to become hypnotized by my own faults."[68]

But it is not in definitions—nor in studies of the Marcellian language of *disponibilité*—that the full significance of the attitude of availability is disclosed. Any adequate understanding of what Marcel describes as availability needs to consider this attitude in the light of his philosophy as a whole. It is possible to see Marcel's entire philosophy, his highly original inquiry into the mystery of being—the mystery of the body, the thou and the sacred—as a description of those concrete modes of being-in-the-world which are the intentionality of availability. The following chapters will show how availability is involved in the life of the body and of community, and in the awareness of the sacred.

[1] *Reflection and Mystery,* p. 201-202.

[2] See *Being and Having,* pp. 69-73 and 123-124. Cf. Gabriel Marcel, *Être et Avoir,* Philosophie de l'Esprit (Paris: Ferdinand Aubier, Éditions Montaigne, 1935), pp. 99-107 and 179-180.

[3] *Reflection and Mystery,* p. 201. The French reads: *Ici intervient une notion qui me paraît capitale mais pour laquelle il n'existe pas de mot satisfaisant en anglais ou même en allemand: je veux dire celle de disponibilité ou d'indisponibilité. (Réflexion et Mystère,* p. 178.)

[4] *Creative Fidelity,* pp. 38, 47, 52-53, 57, 77, 88-89, 134 and 227. Cf. *Invocation,* pp. 55, 67, 75, 106, 119-120, 176 and 291.

[5] See *Homo Viator: Hope,* pp. 23-25, 67 and 146. Cf. Gabriel Marcel, *Homo Viator: Prolégomènes à une Métaphysique de l'Espérance,* Philosophie de l'Esprit (2d. ed.; Paris: Aubier, Éditions Montaigne, 1963), pp. 27-30, 86-193.

[6] *Journal Métaphysique,* p. 164. The philosophical journal or diary Marcel has kept over the years has been published in four forms: the *Journal Métaphysique* (1927), containing notations from 1914-1923; *Être et Avoir* (1935), notations from 1928-1933; *Présence et Immortalité* (1959), notations from 1938-1943; and *Fragments Philosophiques* (1961), notations from 1909-1914.

[7] *Journal Métaphysique,* p. 170.

[8] *Ibid.,* p. 174.

[9] *Ibid.,* pp. 274-275.

[10] *Être et Avoir,* p. 101.

[11] *Invocation,* p. 176.

[12] Gabriel Marcel, *Le Mystère de l'Être,* Vol. II: *Foi et Réalité* (Paris: Aubier, Éditions Montaigne, 1951), p. 78. In this volume, as in the *Journal Métaphysique,* the term *disponibilité* does not occur.

[13] *Ibid.,* p. 80.

[14] *Position et Approches,* p. 83. Cf. *Journal Métaphysique,* pp. 53, 222, 227, 235 and 301; and *Être et Avoir,* pp. 210-211 and 217-218.

[15] *Être et Avoir,* pp. 198-199.

[16] *Ibid.,* pp. 180, 184 and 226.

[17] *Homo Viator: Espérance,* p. 28.

[18] *Position et Approches,* p. 86. Cf. *Être et Avoir,* pp. 105-106.

[19] *Réflexion et Mystère,* p. 178. Marcel's word *empêtre* can mean "embarrassed" and "worried," as well as entangled.

[20] *Reflection and Mystery,* p. 176. This marvellous passage is almost better in Fraser's translation than in the French. It is a very loose translation, but in this case brings forth Marcel's meaning excellently. (Cf. *Réflexion et Mystère,* p. 178.)

[21] *Invocation,* pp. 71-74.

[22] *Être et Avoir,* pp. 99 and 122.

[23] *Invocation,* pp. 76-77. Cf. *Creative Fidelity,* p. 54.

[24] See below, pp. 80-81.

[25] *Position et Approches,* pp. 76 and 85-86. Cf. Gabriel Marcel, *The Philosophy of Existentialism,* trans. by Manya Harari (5th ed.; New York: The Citadel Press, 1965), pp. 34 and 41-42.

[26] *Être et Avoir,* p. 163.

[27] *Homo Viator: Espérance,* p. 31. The figurative meaning of Marcel's word *figer* is "to be very cold" or "to take a stiff attitude."

[28] Gabriel Marcel, *Présence et Immortalité,* Homo Sapiens (Paris: Flammarion, Éditeur, 1959), pp. 145-146.

[29] *Ibid.*

[30] *Ibid.,* pp. 49 and 99.

[31] *Being and Having,* p. 112n.

[32] Gabriel Marcel, *The Mystery of Being,* Vol. II: *Faith and Reality,* trans. by René Hague (6th ed.; Chicago: Henry Regnery Company, 1970), pp. 128-129.

[33] Gabriel Marcel, *Man Against Mass Society,* trans. by G. S. Fraser (Chicago: Henry Regnery Company, 1962), pp. 140-149.

[34] *Ibid.*

[35] *Presence and Immortality,* p. 182.

[36] *Homo Viator: Espérance,* p. 19.

[37] *Ibid.,* pp. 16-20.

[38] *Réflexion et Mystère,* p. 192. Cf. *Reflection and Mystery,* p. 217. This is one of the places where G. S. Fraser's translation is extravagantly loose.

[39] Gabriel Marcel, *The Existential Background of Human Dignity* (Cambridge, Massachusetts: Harvard Univeristy Press, 1963), pp. 34 and 101-102.

[40] *Homo Viator:* Hope, p. 19.

[41] *Ibid.*

[42] *Existentialism,* p. 41.

[43] *Être et Avoir,* p. 100.

[44] *Homo Viator: Hope,* pp. 22-23.

[45] *Reflection and Mystery,* p. 101.

[46] *Faith and Reality,* p. 9.

[47] *Homo Viator: Hope,* pp. 13-18, 32-33, and 61.

[48] *Reflection and Mystery,* p. 8.

[49] *Ibid.*

[50] *Homo Viator: Hope,* p. 23.

[51] *Présence et Immortalité,* p. 125.

[52] *Journal Métaphysique,* p. 282.

[53] *Homo Viator: Espérance,* p. 173.

[54] *Ibid.,* p. 174.

[55] *Réflexion et Mystère,* p. 232.

[56] *Présence et Immortalité,* pp. 120 and 169.

[57] *Invocation,* p. 50.

[58] *Réflexion et Mystère,* pp. 93-95.

[59] *Présence et Immortalité,* pp. 114 and 120-122. The French word *aliéné* can be either a noun or an adjective. As a noun, *aliéné* refers to someone who is mentally unbalanced, a deranged person. As an adjective, it means estranged (or hostilely estranged), as well as unbalanced, mentally. The physical image in which these human meanings of *aliéné* are based is that of transferred capital or property. To have *des capitaux aliénés,* is to no longer have certain capital available: to have given it away or handed it over. (Cf. above, pp. 13-16). The idea of alienation, for Marcel, shows a connection with the attitude of unavailability. To be alienated from

presence—self-presence or the presence of another—is an unavailability. And we are never entirely available in either mode of presence availability brings. "Proust was right: we are not available for ourselves; there is a part of our being to which circumstances, strange and perhaps hardly conceivable, give us sudden access." (*Être et Avoir*, p. 67.)

[60] *Présence et Immortalité*, pp. 114 and 120-122.

[61] *Journal Métaphysique*, p. 280. *Indivision*, in the French, can mean "joint-tenancy." Marcel may have in mind here a concept of a co-dwelling of ourselves and others, a "we," which resides in the self which has conquered dividedness.

[62] *Invocation*, pp. 120 and 41. Cf. *Réflexion et Mystère*, p. 134.

[63] *Invocation*, pp. 120-122.

[64] *Ibid.*, p. 43.

[65] *Ibid.*, p. 123.

[66] *Ibid.*, pp. 71-73.

[67] *Présence et Immortalité*, p. 156.

[68] *Foi et Réalité*, p. 105.

CHAPTER TWO

The Body: Our Initial Availability

The body of a person is an initial availability, the first significance of availability. Every fuller meaning of availability is "grounded" in the meaning it has for the life of our bodies. In the language of the body, rigid, stiffened muscles say: "I will resist any approach on myself. I interpret approach as intrusion!" Loose, supple bodies say we are available. We can be "touched." We are in touch with our own powers and can enjoy the refreshment the presence of another can bring. Our bodies give us a "living room" (*Lebensraum*). Bodily existence is a space we have to welcome presence, or to refuse.

The life of the body is always, already a life which opens onto a surrounding and a social world. A child is with his mother and knows her as answer to his body's needs—coldness giving way to warmth, and wetness to comfort—long before he knows her as another separate being. His body goes before his reflective awareness to give him a being, in the world and with others. The gift precedes his evaluation or his acceptance.

The purpose of this chapter is to explore Marcel's analyses of the body, and to discover there the first, most basic meaning of availability.

I. The Mystery of the Body

On May 7 and 8 of 1914, Marcel notes in his Journal a series of reflections which lead into his phenomenological discoveries on the nature of the body as lived. The insight with which he begins investigation is that "the notion of the body is *not at all univocal.*" We represent our bodies to ourselves in certain ways. How we think the relation of the body and the soul varies along with the conception we form of the nature of the body. Dualism—"the parallelist representation"—for example, depends upon a notion of the body as a "mechanical complexus." The monistic theory, because it thinks of the body as non-extended, can regard the soul as either identical with the body, or as the reality which the body prolongs.[1]

In an article on Marcel, Rudolph Gerber writes that Marcel's phenomenology of the body (which he considers "an original contribution to contemporary philosophy") is developed

> in order to offset the three options around which much of modern philosophy and
> psychology oscillates: to equate matter and mind, to put matter inside mind, or to put

mind inside matter. His intent is to describe the body as it is lived, that is, as an
inseparable and irreducible matrix of all existential structures of consciousness.[2]

Marcel wonders if discussion of the relation of the body and soul does not
await investigation into the reality of the body. His investigation (*recherche*)
will take a stand within experience as lived, and ask how "my body appears to
me myself." What is given to our experience is neither body nor soul, but a
bond, a mysterious unity, bound and realized in acting—for example, in "the
evocation of a gesture, or of an inflection in the voice." Analysis tends to
dissociate aspects which in life are bound up together: as in bodily life, when
thinking and intending are separated, analytically, from the body. "The more
real my experience has been, the less the dissociation between soul and body is
possible."[3] Experience does not give us two terms which need to be related,
but instead "the bond which unites me to my body."[4]

Since Marcel sees this bond as a "mystery," it might be well to introduce
here his classical distinction between "problem" and "mystery." A problem
arises and imposes itself on our attention, because it literally rises up before
our faces. That is, a problem always lies before us in its entirety (problem:
from the Greek *pro-ballo,* an obstacle thrown in our path). A problem need
not involve *us;* anyone—"it doesn't matter who"[5]—could as well approach
the problem and reach for its solution. Techniques can be applied whenever a
problem arises. In fact, the technical attitude, or a cool clinical attitude, is
usually helpful when we are faced with a problem. Surgeons rarely operate on
members of their own families.

A mystery, on the other hand, involves us. We do not fall upon a mystery;
we find ourselves implicated by the mysterious, in a region in which the
distinction, "in me" and "before me," no longer has meaning. This region
should not be confused with what is unknowable: the unknowable is only the
limiting case of the problematic. A mystery may be recognized, a light may
even be shed upon it—or it can be ignored, even actively refused. By definition
a mystery transcends techniques; since we ourselves are involved, we cannot
approach a mystery, or apply our technology to it. Marcel gives the example
of the mystery of evil. We cannot assume a perspective upon evil. An evil
which is only observed (or one which is stated) is no longer evil suffered. What
we suppose we place ourselves before ceases to be evil and becomes an
accident which happens to a mechanical complexus. If this "machine" we
consider is the universe itself, we imagine that we take up the viewpoint of
God, that is, of a God who is only an onlooker. Marcel defines a mystery as "a
problem which encroaches upon its own data, invading them, as it were, and
thereby transcending itself as a simple problem."[6]

We cannot consider the mystery of the body as a problem from which we
can extricate ourselves. I cannot place my body before me (as if it were a thing,
apart from me—and somehow in my way) and ask how can I relate *that* to
myself. "The indivisible unity always inadequately expressed by such phrases
as *I have a body, I make use of my body, I feel my body,* etc., can be neither

analysed nor reconstituted out of precedent elements." What is immediate is given to consciousness as "my body," as "my own presence to myself."[7]

II. "My Body"

It is important to understand that, phenomenologically, reflection on my body "takes the place of the traditional question of the relationship between soul and body."[8] Marcel's meditation on the meaning of "my body" does not intend to be private in any exclusivistic sense. His reflection begins with the personal meaning of "my" body, because he is convinced that we discover the way to truth, not by disengaging ourselves from our situation, but by probing more intensely into it. Like Edmund Husserl, he likes archeological metaphors. He speaks of "excavating—or digging deeply into—my experience (*approfondir mon experience*)."[9] It has never been demonstrated that we even *can* abstract ourselves from our experience.

> To philosophize *sub specie aeterni* may mean something very different from just wiping the slate clean. It may mean devoting myself to understanding my own life as fully as possible. . . . If I try to do so, I shall most likely be led to a strange and wonderful discovery—that the more I raise myself to a really concrete perception of my own experience, the more, by that very act, shall I be attuned to an effective understanding of others, of the experience of others.[10]

Marcel rejects the dilemma which forces us to choose between

> the actual individual man, delivered over to his own states of being and incapable of transcending them, and a kind of generalized thinking as such, what the Germans call *Denken überhaupt*, which would be operative in a sort of Absolute and so claim universal validity for its operations.[11]

He looks for a *common ground* of experience which would be intermediate between the experience of an enclosed self and that of the generalized self. He takes admiration for works of art as one example of an experience people do share in common. There are people, it is true, with whom we cannot communicate the admiration we feel, who have felt nothing, whose attention has never been arrested. Still we know that the impact of a work of art "infinitely transcends the limits of what we call the individual consciousness."[12] Seymour Cain compares Marcel with Karl Jaspers: like Jaspers, Marcel is always making "calls" to fellow travelers on the road, "waiting and hoping for their response, taking this common feeling to indicate that this is the true way into reality."[13]

Marcel thinks of the philosopher as "the man who comes, not without trembling, to share with those who are willing to hear him out a certain experience which it was given him to undergo." The philosopher's function cannot be performed except in "the intimacy of dialogue."[14]

W. E. Hocking (whom Marcel knew well and for whose thought he felt a deep affinity) says of the personal style of Marcel's writing:

Exploration beyond the limits assigned to conceptual thinking will naturally take the form of autobiography. It is most pertinently reported as a private *itinerarium mentis.* But the reason for exploring this region is that the ultimate issues of life are there—the concerns of faith and destiny, the scope of possible experience, the roots of good and evil, the nature of the soul, the mysteries of love and beauty, the sources of obligation. And the ultimate issues of life can never be purely private concerns. Hence the Journal, unable to fulfill it's original intent as jottings for a systematic treatise, must nevertheless be published.[15]

The expression, "my body," is natural to the literary form of personal meditation which Marcel adopts in his lectures, as well as his diaries. His style suits the content of his phenomenological investigations, which are into the nature of bodily existence, and not into the peculiarities of the body of M. Gabriel Marcel.

The body which is a person's body is admittedly difficult to discuss, in French or in English, without falling into language which is either awkward or confusing. Maurice Merleau-Ponty and Paul Ricoeur both use the expression, *le corps propre,* instead of *mon corps* (my body).[16] *Le corps propre* intends to preserve the personal allusion of Marcel's "my" body, yet to indicate the common ground of the corporeity we live.

Marcel's "my body" indicates the bond or link between a being in the first person and the body of this being. This particular body, to which it is appropriate to apply the personal possessive index is not a some-thing (a *quid*), which belongs to someone-in-general. This body which is "mine" cannot be the body of just anyone. When we say "my body" we point out a region of what Marcel calls "hicceity" or hereness.[17] A person's body always has the character of "mineness" or "ownness." It makes a difference that *this* body is some-body (the expression, now almost obsolete, "a body,"—as in "when a body meets a body/comin' through the rye"—expresses a phenomenological intuition). "My body" cannot belong to just anybody. What is there for any body—"it doesn't matter who"—is there for no body in particular. No body in particular would actually mean no body at all.

Marcel's work with the Red Cross, during World War I, involved filling out questionnaires on missing persons. He recalls his impression that the information the questionnaires contained was entirely different from the memories the relatives of the missing persons held. What can be asked and answered of anyone at all, misses what is unique and precious about a living person.[18]

The generalized perspective, which would be everyone's, is a fiction. We cannot, no one of us can, achieve a viewpoint from which all of us could see. Marcel considers it a "naively rationalist idea that you can have a system of affirmation valid for thought *in general,* or for *any consciousness* whatsoever. Such thought as this is the subject of scientific knowledge, a subject which is an idea but nothing else."[19]

When I treat "my body" as if it were interchangeable with the body of "it doesn't matter who," I banish my self to infinity. A personal body loses its character of subjectivity, when it is handled as an object. The object is just that which does not take "me" into account. Marcel takes the object in its etymological sense, as something thrown in our path, before us in our way. (The etymology is the same as that of the problem.) To the extent it does not take an "I" into account, a body is not a personal body, not your body, not "my body." It is the non-objectivity of the personal body, in this sense, that Marcel's "my body" intends to preserve.[20]

When we think of our bodies as objects, separate from our selves, we represent them as instruments which we use. It can be convenient for us to use our bodies, in this manner. Marcel cites the example of "the emancipated girl who tells her parents that her body belongs to her, that she can do what she pleases with it."[21] A deeper reflection shows that this representation is false.

Every instrument or tool is a way of prolonging or strengthening a power of the body. This instrumental relation is as true of a microscope as it is of a spade.[22] For us to make use of tools, there must be a community of nature between tools and the personal bodies which use them. But if we represent the body which uses the tool as itself an instrument, do we not imagine a sort of physical soul to which we give back the very powers the tool prolongs? If these powers themselves are considered as instruments, then we are engaged in an infinite regress. An instrument can only be on the condition that it specifies or extends something which is not an instrument. We can think of our bodies as instruments only if we take for granted the existence of a body that is not an instrument.[23] Roger Troisfontaines observes that to consider the body as an instrument placed between ourselves and other things is to construct a metaphor in reverse. Instrumentality is a construction on the analogy of "my body," and not vice versa.[24]

Our relation to our bodies is characterized by an essential ambiguity. We are inclined to treat our bodies as some thing we have: an instrument, an apparatus external to ourselves. Marcel says that Americans periodically have themselves "checked up" in clinics. The hospital functions as the mechanic's garage. (A doctor once said to me: "When I am sick, I want a good mechanic.") On the other hand, something in us rises up against the pretense of the technician who goes through his operations on our bodies, as if *we* were not there. The protest is spontaneous: "My body is not something that I have; *I am my body*."[25]

There are human experiences which the expression, "I have a body," or "I make use of my body," cannot translate. The formula, "I am my body," has primarily a negative meaning: "*It is not true to say* that I am not my body."[26]

Marcel suggests that materialism can be understood as an effort to organize this protest. He does not want, however, to interpret "I am my body" in a materialist sense. The meaning of "I am my body" is the denial of the gap between ourselves and our bodies—that gap which opens up whenever we consider our bodies as instruments. The denial does not intend to identify the body of a person with the body of materialism. The life of our bodies cannot be identified with this object others see and touch—and will still see and touch when we die. This body which is some thing for others is other than our selves. We can adopt a position from which to judge this body, and it is true to say that we sometimes fail to recognize ourselves in it.[27]

Marcel recognizes limiting cases of illness or injury in which we can no longer say, "I am my body":

> My body is only properly mine to the degree to which I am able to control it. But here, too, there is a limit, an inner limit; if as a consequence of some illness, I lose all control of my body, it tends to cease to be *my* body, for the very profound reason that, as we say in the common idiom, I am "no longer myself."[28]

Marcel can also speak of "mere bodies occupying a certain share of space in the *Lebensraum* in which we have to maintain our own share of space and through which we have to thrust our way."[29] (At three in the morning in New York City, the Broadway Express headed uptown is full of "mere bodies.")

Our bodies, so far as they are subject to accident, can and should be treated as "mere bodies." If we are knocked unconscious, we want to be taken to the hospital. For certain purposes, we sometimes will the body as object—as sex object or object of manipulation. We can exhibit our bodies to attract sexually, or to mesmerize. We have to take proper care of our bodies, as we do any thing we own. "My body needs to be nourished, to be exercised, to be rested; my body which is in no way privileged with regard to other things.[30]

This body which occupies no position of privilege before the other things, which "I consider as a body among an unlimited number of other bodies,"[31] Marcel calls the "body-object" (*le corps-objet*). The personal body (*mon corps*) which is not assimilable to that "body-object," he calls the "body-subject" (*le corps-sujet*).[32] The body-subject is "the body insofar as it is inaccessible to the manipulations, real or ideal, to which the scientist can or must submit extended things."[33] The body-subject identifies the living bond between ourselves and our bodies, "the *situation* of a being who appears to himself as fundamentally, and not accidentally, connected to his body."[34] Or the body-subject alludes to the essential ambiguity of the body as lived—"the body I am without being able logically to identify myself with it."[35] We live our bodies in two irreducibly different modalities. The two modes are indissoluable, as complementary experiences of ourselves: "I am my body," and "I make use of my body."[36]

III. "My Body" as Landmark

The distinction between body-subject and body-object throws light on Marcel's enigmatic notion of the "existing object, that which in my body (inasmuch as it is mine) transcends objectivity."[37] This is a difficult notion, but an important one—since it is here the movement from "my body" to the world becomes effective. "There is between me and everything that exists a relation (the word is entirely improper) of the same type as the one which unites me to my body. This amounts to saying that my body is *in sympathy with things.*"[38] If there were no sympathy of nature between ourselves and our bodies, how could we affirm that anything exists? We can only pay attention to whatever affects us in some way. Merleau-Ponty gives the example of the blind man's stick. The resistance of things to his stick gives him a world. His world is the pressure at the end of his stick. The world, for him, is how his stick feels the touch of the things. And since the stick is the prolongation of his body (the hand, in this instance), it is true to say that the world is the way his body feels.[39] The affection of our bodies in the world is the medium (or mediation) through which we direct our attentive activity.[40] Things and other beings affect our bodies through an *Urgefühl*—a being affected which is fundamental. This *Urgefühl* can in no way be known, precisely because it *is* fundamental—the foundation of any other "feeling." Thus our bodies are the necessary condition for any object to come to our attention. Our bodies—so far as they are "felt" or lived—cannot themselves be objects, since it is they who know objects.[41]

From the objective point of view, the body is one thing among others, it occupies no privileged position. But as interposed between myself and the objects of my attention, this body which is mine appears as privileged object, my landmark (*repère*) upon the world, a living center. That I can have a world at all means that I have a "place," a position from which my life can venture out among the things surrounding me. My body gives me such a place, a position of privilege from which I take the measure of the things of the world and familiarize myself with what is strange and other. Everything which is for me passes through my body. This is Marcel's idea of "an absolute interposition of my body."[42] He does not intend to question the reality of things, he only intends to specify that their existence is apprehended in our bodies, and because we are embodied. "My body is . . . at one time the existent-type and more profoundly still the landmark on all existing things."[43]

IV. Sensation

The idea of the interposition of the body is obscure and abstract. Marcel's analysis of sensation or "feeling" and its connection with "my body" will perhaps make it more concrete. Marcel writes: "It is quite clear that to pay attention to something is always to lend attention to the self as feeling (*sentant*)."[44] I have translated the last word in this quotation as "feeling," because this is how Marcel's translators usually handle his use of the French *sentir* and its variants.[45] "Feeling," as a translation of *sentir*, should be unloaded of connotations Marcel does not intend the French to carry. Richard Zaner points out that "to feel," in English, can mean "to touch," and that Marcel nowhere uses either *toucher* or *tâter*.[46] *Sentir* is not "feeling" as a touching. Neither does *sentir*, as Marcel uses it, mean "mere feeling." The "problem of sensation," as it is usually discussed, reduces feeling to a "mere feeling." A "feeling" describes an interior state of consciousness which may have no reference to any world beyond consciousness. A "sensation," on the other hand, is an impression the world makes on us, as a seal impresses a mass of wax. Marcel suspends this distinction between sensation and feeling. He wants to get a fresh look at what "to sense" means. ("To sense" or "sensing" might be a better translation of *sentir* than "feeling.") He wants to replace the "problem of sensation" with the "mystery of sensing (*sentir*)."[47] Marcel's language retains the vague "sense" of *sentir* which ordinary language expresses—as, for example, when he writes of his presentiment of World War II: "I sensed (*je sentais*) a catastrophe coming which would mean the fall of everything we love."[48] In English, we could have said either "I felt . . ." or "I sensed . . . ."

The substantive form of *sentir* which Marcel uses is *le sentir,* a word which is evidently his own construction—a noun formed on an infinitive. "Sensing," for Marcel, indicates an experiencing, in a broadened sense of the term experience: a prehension or apprehension.[49] "To sense (*sentir*) is to be affected in a certain manner; and we should ask whether the very ambiguity of the word has not a profound and very real foundation."[50]

Sensing is a modification in our bodies of the way we are in the world. It is a given mood or modulation of bodily existence. *Le sentir* expresses a sense we have for our bodies, and a sense of our bodies for the world. Sensing is a reach towards . . . , a centrifugal motion, from the center of our embodiment. In a notation in his Journal, in which the term "feeling" occurs in the English, Marcel writes:

> Elsewhere I have identified the existent with the body's possibility of locating it. But we must see that it is a question of the *sensible locating* [*repérage sensible*], and not only of identification, . . . the center, or if we wish, the immediate experience from which these locatings emerge [*l'experience immédiate d'ou partent ces continus*], is not a simple "feeling," is linked in a way which is unthinkable . . . with the mood [*représentation*] of an object which is my body.[51]

Marcel offers a critique of two usual approaches to the "problem of sensation." The first thinks of sensation as the translation of a physical event, as for instance, the image inscribed on the retina. Marcel asks if a translation in this case is even conceivable. A translation always replaces one datum with another, according to a certain code whose definiteness is more or less precise. The *initial* datum of sensation, according to this translation hypothesis, is the physical event. But the physical event is exactly what is not given to consciousness. We cannot see the image on the retina. This image belongs to the perceptual world, to the consciousness of the other. It is not given to us, and it is unthinkable that we could translate what in no way is given to *us.*

The second approach thinks of sensation as the transcription, transmission, and re-transcription of a message. At the origin of transmission, there is some message analogous to what is given to us in sensation. (A flower takes an obscure delight in existing and by its perfume communicates its mood to us?) The hidden (mixed) metaphor behind this hypothesis is that sensation is somehow like the communication which takes place in radio or television broadcasting.[52] Ricoeur notices that the interpretation of sensation as a message is linked to that of the body as instrument (ourselves as telephones, televisions . . .).[53]

Marcel wonders what is the point in telling ourselves "this little story about a so-called message." Everyone admits that the "shaking of the atmosphere" is finally transcribed into sensation, anyhow. So, after we have told the story, we are left with the original "problem": what is sensation?[54] The "story" about a message explains nothing; it only pushes the problem—or the mystery—back one step further. Finally, it is always *somebody* who reads, translates or interprets a message.

As John O'Malley says in his essay on Marcel, the essential weakness of any analogy which compares sensation to a camera or radio, is that the meaning of words like "signal," "response" and "message" is based upon the life of our bodies. It is a "re-analogy" for us to interpret the sensation of our bodies according to the "communication" of the instruments our bodies use and construct.[55] Every communication, every interpretation, supposes a mode of sensing as its basis. Marcel notes: "To sense is not to communicate. . . . To sense is not to receive, but to participate immediately."[56]

Marcel does not question a physiological explanation of sensation. Something travels between our bodies and the flower garden, whose scent comes to us—something which the scientist correctly studies as a disturbance of particles in the air. The disturbance or wave somehow gets translated into olfactory language—everyone admits this. There is no doubt that a physical event takes place, that something is "sent" and something "received."[57] The abortion of the physical event is enough to prevent sensation from happening. Blindness is the end of seeing; drugs can alter our perceptions, strangely and radically. Marcel does not want to deny any of this, only to question whether this something which is transmitted and received (and sometimes intercepted or missed) is sensation. And he reminds us that sensation can only be experienced when the body adopts a given attitude, or is available in a certain way. A woman who can sleep through any kind of street noise may awake immediately when her child cries out in the night. "Here we rediscover everything I have said about the ambiguities which the idea of *my body* conceals. As I said, we must choose between treating the body as an object among other objects, or as the mysterious condition of objectivity in general."[58]

From the point of view of the body-object, sensation can be a communication. For the body-subject, sensation—if it cannot be described as a message—can only be intelligible as "an immediate participation of what we commonly call the subject in a surroundings from which no veritable frontiers separate him."[59] Marcel does not use the word *participation* in a Platonic sense. Participation implies the notion of a common element or milieu, but the milieu is not an Idea or Ideal Object. Participation is a sharing in or a being together within a common creation or task (marriage, parenthood . . .); or it is an immersion in an "atmosphere," as in an atmosphere of understanding or celebration. Merleau-Ponty says that sensation is a communion.[60] For Marcel, sensation is a direct participation, and it must be understood from above, from the higher forms of participation: worship, love, the communion of saints and sinners. The immediate presence to the world which sensation affords cannot be understood from below, since "to sense" (*sentir*) is the fundamental participation, our original (in the sense of the German *ursprünglich*) being with the world—our first availability.[61]

The personal body is our initial availability, because sensation opens us immediately upon a world. Availability is the meaning of sensation for the body-subject. The body is given to immediate experience in two ways: as the object of touching, feeling, seeing . . .; and as the concrete expression, the real-ization of ourselves, so far as we are in the world. The body is at once an object of perception and the foundation of every act of perceiving. It is this essential and mysterious ambiguity of the body which is somebody's which gives it the character of an initial or fundamental availability. The body manifests our identity and is the condition of our identification and communication with otherness. Others are given to us, we give ourselves away in a touch or in a smile, sometimes in a scent. Our bodies present and "presence" us to the world. It is difficult to imagine how we could be present to anyone without our bodies.

A world of spirit in which the identification of beings was no longer possible would be a contradiction, both logically and ontologically. Beings which could not identify each other, or manifest themselves to each other, would have lost personal and spiritual being. It is essential that persons have bodies (or something like bodies) to know and recognize one another by. St. Paul must have been struck by this phenomenological intuition when he spoke of the "spiritual bodies" of the Resurrection. Personal life needs embodiment for its realization; without embodiment availability goes nowhere.[62] The spirit "only constitutes itself effectively *as* spirit on condition of becoming flesh." The example Marcel gives is of the adopted child. Adoption, when it is accomplished, is "a kind of grafting of the flesh onto the spirit." The personal body is the milieu or point of juncture of the vital and the spiritual.[63]

Marcel writes of "my body" as an "interposition." My body is in sympathy with things, and I am in sympathy with my body as I act and live in the world. To say that "my body is my way of being in the world" implies both relations: of myself to my body and of my body to the world. It is in my "feeling" (an *Urgefühl*) of my body as in sympathy with things that the movement from my body to the world is effected. The mystery of the bond which unites us to our bodies is one with the mystery through which our being is a being-in-the-world. We cannot look behind the act, whether it be accident or grace, by which our birth thrusts us into a world.

Specifically, it is through sensation, or sensing, that our "reach" toward otherness—the intent of availability—is actualized. Bodily availability is always a question of a "location" (*repérage*) which is at once sensible and sentient.

Because the ground of our availability is sensual and bodily, availability is an opening upon the world which is also a closing. Our bodies are an opening *because* they are a closing. The human body is a finitude and a facticity; it is also our point of view, that particular vision of the universe which, uniquely, is given to us. It is possible for us to see our flesh (the world of our embodiment) as a limit and restriction imposed upon us; or we can interpret "flesh" as a milieu of communication and communion, that region of the cosmos where word and presence become incarnate. For example, words need the body—teeth, tongue, throat, pallet, hands—to be articulated. Thinking, consciousness, intending (the whole infinite world of meaning) are inseparable from their realization by means of word and "flesh." Similarly, presence needs to manifest itself, and needs further some means of visibility and tangibility for its manifestation. Presence requires something (some embodiment) by which it can make itself known. The gnostic (of every age) has distrusted flesh because he feared (claustrophobically) an imprisonment in skin or a loss of spirituality in the carnal. The gnostic view of flesh is still possible, but only possible if the human meaning of the body as an initial availability is forgotten. If we have only our view of the universe, that view can disclose for us a vision. If every perspective implies the horizons which limit our sight, still the horizon is a structure which the expansion of perspective (through, for example, motility or empathy) may broaden to inifinity. We may resent our incarnation as a wound inflicted on us at birth; or we may accept it as an original gift, laden with promises.[64]

Our bodies can be for us the way of our incarnation into distance and deep intimacies, and also our first openness to the incarnation of the sacred. Bergson wrote that our bodies extend to the stars, because they are coextensive with our "reach."[65] For Marcel, being incarnate is the landmark (*repère*) on metaphysical reflection, as well as "the central given of metaphysics."[66] Marcel saw, already in 1914, that a theory of participation leads to a "new metaphysics based on religion." This new metaphysics would be what he calls a "sensualist metaphysics."[67]

The next two chapters will explore the possibility that such a metaphysics begins when the presence of another "touches" us. Marcel, more than once, quoted a sentence from E. M. Forster's *Howards End:* "It is private life that holds out the mirror to infinity: personal intercourse, and that alone, that ever hints at a personality beyond our daily vision."[68]

[1]*Journal,* pp. 124-127.

[2]Rudolph J. Gerber, "Marcel and the Experiential Road to Metaphysics," *Philosophy Today,* XXII, No. 4/4 (1968), 271.

[3]*Journal,* pp. 126, 248, and 261.

[4]*Homo Viator: Hope,* p. 69.

[5]Marcel's category of the *"n'importe qui."* See *Journal Métaphysique,* pp. 204, 305 and 315; and *Position et Approches,* p. 50.

[6]*Existentialism,* pp. 18-19. Cf. *Being and Having,* pp. 100-101; and *Reflection and Mystery,* pp. 260-261.

[7]*Existentialism,* p. 19; and *Journal,* pp. 260 and 335.

[8]*Human Dignity,* p. 45.

[9]*Invocation,* pp. 23-24.

[10]*Faith and Reality,* p. 7.

[11]*Reflection and Mystery,* p. 11.

[12]*Ibid.,* p. 12.

[13]Seymour Cain, *Gabriel Marcel,* Studies in Modern European Literature and Thought (New York: Hillary House Publishers, Ltd., 1963), p. 108.

[14]*Human Dignity,* pp. 168-169.

[15]W. E. Hocking, "Marcel and the Ground Issues of Metaphysics," *Philosophy and Phenomenological Research,* XIV, No. 4 (1954), 440.

[16]Maurice Merleau-Ponty, *Phénoménologie de la Perception,* Bibliotèque des Idèes (10th ed.; Paris: Librairie Gallimard, 1945), pp. 114 and 123. Paul Ricoeur, *Philosophie de la Volonté,* Tome I: *Le Volontaire et l'Involontaire,* Philosophie de l'Esprit (Paris: Aubier, Éditions Montaigne, 1950), pp. 14-15.

[17]*Journal,* p. 129.

[18]Gabriel Marcel, "Vers une Ontologie Concrète," *Encyclopédie Française,* 1957, XIX, 19.14-3 and 19.14-4.

[19]*Being and Having,* p. 120.

[20]*Journal,* pp. 305, 314, and 316; and *Being and Having,* p. 19; and *Reflection and Mystery,* p. 57.

[21]*Human Dignity,* p. 98.

[22]This concept of the tool is usually attributed to McLuhan, but it appears in Marcel's Journal as early as 1920.

[23]*Journal,* pp. 245, 255, and 275. Cf. *Presence and Immortality,* p. 234.

[24]Troisfontaines, *Existence,* I, 184.

[25]*Presence and Immortality,* p. 234; and *Being and Having,* p. 109; and *Journal,* p. 208.

[26]*Journal,* p. 260.

[27]*Journal,* pp. 332-333; and *Reflection and Mystery,* p. 124; and *Human Dignity,* p. 46.

[28]*Reflection and Mystery,* p. 119.

[29]*Ibid.,* p. 170.

[30]*Presence and Immortality,* p. 131.

[31]*Invocation,* p. 31.

[32]*Réflexion et Mystère,* pp. 116-117.

[33]*Human Dignity,* p. 46.

[34]*Réflexion et Mystère,* p. 117.

[35]*Invocation,* p. 39.

[36]*Journal Métaphysique,* p. 21.

[37]*Journal,* pp. 273-274.

[38]*Journal Métaphysique,* p. 265.

[39]Maurice Merleau-Ponty, *Phenomenology of Perception,* trans. by Colin Smith, International Library of Philosophy and Scientific Method (4th ed.; London: Routledge & Kegan Paul, 1967), p. 152. Cf. Paul Ricoeur, *Freedom and Nature: The Voluntary and the Involuntary,*

trans. by Erazim Kohák, Northwestern University Studies in Phenomenology and Existential Philosophy (Evanston: Northwestern University Press, 1966), p. 110.

[40]In his Journal, Marcel distinguishes between two analogous relations which give us access to the world: the one, between ourselves and our bodies, he calls "sympathetic mediation"; the other, between our bodies and the world, he calls "instrumental mediation." The two depend upon each other in a complementary way. It is the very "antinomy" of personal life that instrumental and sympathetic mediation are only exercised at once.

Marcel probably found this distinction more confusing than helpful: he never used it after 1920. During this same time, in one of his discussions of telepathy, he notes that telepathy is only a particular case of the sympathetic mediation which makes instrumental mediation possible. (Journal, pp. 246-248.)

[41]Ibid., pp. 247, 274 and 255.

[42]Être et Avoir, p. 156. Cf. Journal, p. 154.

[43]Journal Métaphysique, p. 261.

[44]Ibid., p. 240.

[45]Cf. Invocation, p. 43, with Creative Fidelity, p. 28; and cf. Réflexion et Mystère, p. 119, with Reflection and Mystery, p. 129.

[46]Richard M. Zaner, The Problem of Embodiment: Some Contributions to a Phenomenology of the Body, Phaenomenologica, No. 3 (The Hague: Martinus Nijhoff, 1964), p. 35.

[47]Invocation, p. 36.

[48]Ibid., p. 159.

[49]Réflexion et Mystère, pp. 37 and 120.

[50]Journal Métaphysique, p. 185. Cf. Journal, p. 187.

[51]Journal Métaphysique, pp. 304-305. Cf. Journal, p. 315. Cf. also Refléxion et Mystère, pp. 117 and 120, with Reflection and Mystery, pp. 125 and 128.

[52]Journal, pp. 277-278 and 327-328.

[53]Ricoeur, Marcel, p. 98.

[54]Reflection and Mystery, p. 131.

[55]John B. O'Malley, The Fellowship of Being: An Essay on the Concept of Person in the Philosophy of Gabriel Marcel (The Hague: Martinus Nijhoff, 1966), p. 88.

[56]Journal Métaphysique, pp. 250-251.

[57]Human Dignity, p. 44.

[58]Journal Métaphysique, p. 271.

[59]Ibid., p. 322.

[60]Merleau-Ponty, Perception, p. 212.

[61]Invocation, pp. 39-40. For a fuller discussion of participation, see below, pp. 90-103.

[62]Journal, pp. 255-256. Cf. Homo Viator: Hope, p. 26.

[63]Reflection and Mystery, p. 249.

[64]I mean incarnation (as distinguished from "the Incarnation") here as Marcel frequently uses the term, in a sense free from all theological implications. Incarnation is "the situation of a being who appears to himself to be linked fundamentally and not accidentally to his or her body." (Reflection and Mystery, p. 124.)

[65]Henri Bergson, The Two Sources of Morality and Religion, trans. by R. Ashley Audra and Cloudesley Brereton, with the assistance of W. Horsfall Carter, Doubleday Anchor Books (Garden City, New York: Doubleday & Company, Inc., 1935), p. 258.

[66]Être et Avoir, p. 11, and Invocation, p. 19.

[67]Journal, pp. 5-6 and 316.

[68]Ibid., p. 129, quoting Howards End (4th ed.; New York: Alfred A. Knopf, 1944), chap. x. Cf. Creative Fidelity, p. 147.

CHAPTER THREE
Availability For Communion

Behind the description of the personal body, at least in the French phase of the phenomenological movement, lies the inspiration of Bergson's distinction between the open and the closed.[1] Marcel, more than once, recognizes this inspiration.

> I have often said that the distinction between the open and the closed introduced by Bergson in *The Two Sources of Morality and Religion* has undoubtedly a greater importance than he suspected.[2]

The nature of a person's body as opening (our initial availability) is no bleak and vacant openness, but a way—in the sense of the French *sens*.[3] The personal body is a meaning, its meaning lies in the direction of availability. The "sense" of availability begins to be indicated when it is seen as availability for communion. Troisfontaines locates "the ordering principle" of Marcel's work in his "search into the sense *(sens)* of ontological communion."[4] The purpose of this chapter will be to follow Marcel in the direction availability leads us, into the fullness of communion.

I. Communion

In a parenthesis which Marcel probably added to his *Metaphysical Journal* after he had read Heidegger (as he had not when the Journal was first published—in 1927, the same year *Sein und Zeit* came out), he says that communion is an equivalent of *Mitsein* (being with or "with-being").[5] Although he nowhere gives a strict definition of communion, he obviously borrows the word from the Christian tradition: the celebration of the sacrament seems to function for him as the model for understanding what communion means. The ordinary forms of communion are understood in comparison with its profounder forms, and not vice versa. "Communion has a radically unintelligible character for one who is not a communicant."[6]

Marcel had used the word communion already in the first working notes he published under the title, the *Metaphysical Journal* (1914-1923); the word appears more frequently in the most recent collection of his notes, published as *Presence and Immortality* (1938-1943).[7] Communion is the word I have chosen as suited to bring together related analyses of Marcel: the meditation on the preposition "with," the descriptions of presence, intersubjectivity[8] and participation in being. When we see the connections between these various analyses, we get insights into how Marcel uses the word communion, and into how availability admits us to forms of communion which can be increasingly profound.

Communion is a *Mitsein*. The situation the word "with" describes is not one of simple location in space and time. The objects (utensils) we use, according to Marcel, can be "alongside" or "beside," but not "with" each other, as persons are. The distinction is not so obvious in the English as in the French. In English, we can say that my car is "with" yours in the parking lot. In French, neither *chez* nor *avec* is ever applied to objects; another preposition such as *de* or *parmi* must be used when an inanimate object is intended. The preposition *chez* is even difficult to translate into English; it includes connotations of a familiarity—sometimes a dwelling within a domesticated space—which the word "with" barely expresses. If I am invited *chez* Charles, I am welcomed into his home. If I agree *chez* Proust, I find myself in his company, sharing a certain idea. A common bond is created with the word *chez*.

Marcel's point is a phenomenological one. The preposition "with" can express various intensities of intimacy—or in English no intimacy at all. Our cars are together in the parking lot, but certainly not in any intimate sense. On the other hand, we remain "close" to friends whom we have not seen in years, and we would not hesitate to say they are closer to us than the pharmacy down the street, or the couple next door. The language we use to express togetherness can be deceptive. The level of reality the preposition "with" refers to is sometimes "low and barren." People together in a subway car or in a crowd on the street rarely see each other, rarely speak. Sometimes an incident occurs which modifies this situation, and people are with each other in another way: as in the power blackout in the Northeast in 1969.[9]

The situation of meeting a stranger on a train illustrates the possible degrees of intimacy. At first, I address him only to get from him certain information (his name, where he lives, what his occupation is . . .). I may become aware as we talk that he hears the words I say, but does not hear *me*. He relays my words back to me, comments on them, but what returns to me is unrecognizable. This other, "by a singular phenomenon, interposes himself between me and my reality." He can make me a stranger to myself, so that in some way I no longer understand myself or adhere to my words as mine.[10]

A communication of an authentic but superficial sort is established; information is exchanged. A communication of this sort falls short of communion. There is nothing here to bind the other to myself: I will continue to consider him as "that man," another being who has little or nothing to do with me. But if in the course of our conversation we discover that there exists between us a certain community of interest and experience (we have visited some of the same places, or we have friends in common), then this "other" who was "he" or "him" becomes for me a "thou," and perhaps he addresses me as a "thou."[11] "A felt unity takes shape between us," a com-union.[12]

II. Presence

Communion can also be understood as a sharing or enjoyment of presence. Presence, Marcel knows, cannot be defined or circumscribed. Troisfontaines points out that the reason it is difficult to bring presence to the level of discourse is that "we *are* this personal world, we do not see it."[13] This recalls Marcel's understanding of mystery; presence is a mystery. If we are to "approach" presence, we have to dismantle the notion we spontaneously form of another being as an object.[14] An object is always enclosed within its own limits and cannot be present within ours. The object cannot reach out to us. We can see an object and touch it, but it cannot touch us—it is inanimate. It can no more open out to us as presence than can a corpse. "Presence signifies more and something other than being-there; in all strictness, we cannot say of an object that it is present."[15] In fact, the more real a being becomes for us (the more present) the less we think we can see around him.[16] We assume that living beings conceal more than objects. We know that the more *personal* life is, the greater are the depths hidden beneath the surfaces revealed to us.

A presence refuses to allow us to posit it in a definite region of space, as if it were a "solid, flawless mass" (a Parmenidean sphere). The space of presence is more like musical space than geometric space: it fills the room, overflows the person, plays between persons or lingers around our persons. Presence goes out from one person to another and will be the possession of no one.[17] Ricoeur says that it is "most often only a lure, a promise, sometimes only a nostaligia scarcely noticed."[18]

Presence cannot be grasped as an object, but only glimpsed or alluded to, in simple and immediate experiences which the philosopher usually neglects. It is undeniable that some people reveal themselves to us as present (at our disposal) whenever we are ill or need someone to confide in. There are others who do not give us this feeling at all; we suspect they are looking at us, analytically, as only another interesting case. There is a way of listening which is a lending of ourselves, and another way of listening which is a refusal of ourselves.[19] We can be in the room with someone, sitting very close to him. We can see and hear him, we could reach out and touch him if we dared. He is here with us, but is nevertheless not present. He may be immeasurably farther from us at this moment than a loved one who is miles away, even one who has died. We can communicate with this person; he is neither deaf nor blind. But something is missing—he is not *present*. We know whether someone is present or not, because when the other is present, he renews us in some way and makes us more fully ourselves than we would have been alone. It is not so much what the other says, but that he puts *himself* into his words and sustains his words by all he is.[20]

These experiences in which presence is known show "an essentially gratuitous quality"; we must acknowledge, says Marcel, that they happen as a grace (gift) or something close to it. (To not have the gift for presence is no disgrace.) Presence cannot be taught, as a social virtue; it is beyond know-how.

Gestures and grins can be taught, but not presence.[21] Presence, as a gift, implies no impoverishment to the giver, for it is presented to the one who manifests it, as well as to the one who receives it.[22] Presence "reveals itself immediately and unmistakably in a look, a smile, an accent, a handshake."[23]

It comes to the same thing whether we say a being is given to us as a presence or as a being: he is not a being for us if he is not a presence. Through presence the other comes to me. Marcel would like to say that presence is an "influx" of being, if the word influx could be "purified" of its spatial connotation—as a saline solution is purified as liquid is added to it. The presence of another enters us. "He is not only before me; he is also within me, or rather these categories are surmounted; they are no longer meaningful."[24] There is literally an in-fluence of the other to us, although in no spatial sense. Ricoeur comments that what Marcel, the poet, calls "presence," Marcel, the philosopher-dramatist, calls the passage from the closed to the open.[25]

We cannot interpret presence except as a will seeking to disclose itself to us. "At the root of presence, there is a being who takes me into consideration, who is regarded as taking me into account." Presence breaks forth as a response to the act by which we open ourselves to receive. Presence belongs only to the being who assumes the attitude of availability, to the one who can give himself freely and can empty himself of obstacles which would stand in the way of its revelation.[26] This is what Troisfontaines means when he writes that "the 'thou' as value, as *being,* is a function of my interior availability."[27] Availability is "the act by which we incline ourselves towards a presence." We grasp at an object, seize it to manipulate and to control it. Manipulation of a presence "is excluded in principle"—or perhaps forbidden. Presence can be welcomed or rebuffed, but it "lies beyond the grasp of any possible prehension."[28]

III. Intersubjectivity

Presence rises forth from a ground of intersubjectivity. In his contribution to the *Encyclopédie Française,* Marcel discusses intersubjectivity as an "opening" from one subject to another. The term, "intersubjectivity," does not appear in Marcel's earlier writings—in the *Metaphysical Journal* or in *Being and Having.* Marcel begins to use it during the period of his Gifford Lectures (he likely picked it up from his reading of the German phenomenologists). He uses the word because it seems to fit a "central intuition" of his, around which "the first insights on fidelity, on witness, at the same time as on hope, are developed." The concept of intersubjectivity, in Marcel's thought, is one way he uses language to suggest that region or "zone of mystery" in which the distinction of "before me" (*devant moi*) and "in me" (*en moi*) loses significance. But it would be too simplistic to say that intersubjectivity means an identity of the subject and object of personal intercourse.

> It is rather a question of realising that the more we raise ourselves to the apprehension of
> spiritual reality, or of reality as spiritual, the more we are grounded in the affirmation

that the distinction between the subject and the object is insignificant, and even, in the limiting case, tends to vanish. But this is not to say that the subject and object are identical. Rather, it signifies that the categories of subject and object no longer reveal and are no longer adequate.[29]

Marcel's thought does not assume, in the Cartesian fashion, an "I" as a primitive and self-evident datum of experience. The belief we commonly and practically hold in the existence of others is not a result of reasoning by analogy. For Marcel, a "we-territory" (the territory of intersubjectivity) is more original in experience than an "I-territory." We constitute ourselves as interiority, as we recognize the reality of the other. It makes no sense for us to admit that the ego is encapsulated by skin. How do we know, for example, what thoughts are our own and what ones we owe to the in-fluence of others? Are we really able to footnote each thought we have (or each action, for that matter), as if we knew for certain that its source lay either within us or outside ourselves?[30] "A simple phrase accidentally hit upon can be for the fertile mind the incentive or point of crystallization for a whole series of complicated reflections. This simple fact is sufficient to show why the expression *my* philosophy is practically meaningless."[31] In Marcel's *Le Quator en Fa Dièse,* Roger cries, "Ah! it is frightful to think that I have not been loved for myself"; and Claire replies, "Yourself? Himself? Where does a personality commence?"[32]

The conception of the "I" as a monad, independent and without real connection with other beings, is false in two senses: it is strange to say, but we are never alone, nor are we one. Phenomenologically, the "we" reveals itself as more profound and more stable than the "I" (witness, for example, the return of the prodigal son). Arguments, quarrels appear as a rupture, as an assertion of self-interest or prejudice against an intersubjectivity already established. Such an intersubjectivity is, of course, always an expression of intimacy and availability, and not of constraint.[33] When the bonds of intimacy are broken or disrupted, then the "ego" appears to consciousness as independent and alone. "One day he discovers that she is being unfaithful to him."

> From the core of the *us* I subtract the element that is *not-me* and call it *thou*. This element has an automatic tendency to take on the character of the *him*. And it is only in the measure in which I succeed in re-living this experience of intimacy after the event that I am able to resist this temptation.[34]

The intersubjective is an "element from which the ego seems to emerge like an island rising from the waves." The function of intersubjectivity, for Marcel, is that of background or horizon against which the "I" and the "thou" stand out. This horizon function of intersubjectivity constitutes the condition of possibility of communion, of conversation, of community—of every communication. It constitutes also the radically mysterious nature of intersubjectivity. Intersubjectivity is a "community deeply rooted in ontology, without which human relations would be unintelligible." This community is "deeply felt"; it cannot be pointed out as if it were this thing here or there. Marcel says it has its own peculiar quality, a "spiritual quality."[35]

Hocking writes, in his article on Marcel, that "the most compact expression of our elemental intersubjectivity is, no doubt, the casual 'Here we are.'" He also writes:

> If one knows such an experience, one needs no argument. If one hopes for it, the saying is pertinent, "Thou couldst not seek me hadst thou not already found me"; for if there were no experience of "we" there could be no idea of "we."[36]

The metaphors through which we gain understanding are usually optical ones: images of physical space, pictures which words offer us. An understanding of intersubjectivity requires another kind of metaphor—a musical one, for example. Musical "metaphors" are not pictures so much as "moods" (in the Heideggerian sense of a mood: a way of feeling or finding ourselves affected in a certain time and place). We cannot stand back from musical space; the only way we can know the space of music is to get into it—"into the mood," as we say. Marcel speaks of "the world in which I move when I am improvising on the piano" as "a world in which everything is in communication, in which everything is bound together." In fact, improvisation, or even jazz—variation on a theme—is possible only because in this world everything *is* bound together: one theme naturally, of its own as it were, calls forth another.

> Music, or musical consciousness, appears as completely transcending the realm of Eris—that of arguments and disputes in which everyone is revealed as being fundamentally selfish, harboring demands and claims on others. Thus music appears as the sensuous, and at the same time supra-sensuous, expression of that intersubjectivity which opens philosophic reflection to the discovery of the concrete *thou* and *us*.[37]

The "area" of our life which is intersubjective is also like the area psychology designates as the unconscious. We can say that what Freud discovered was a new myth—but only on pain of denying the force of the unconscious on our waking, watching life. We have never seen this new world Freud discovered, as we have never seen the world of music (or of intersubjectivity); but we know of its existence, because we have visited it in our dreams and sojourned there through our neuroses. Like musical space, the space of the unconscious is relatively boundary-less. Here "it is no longer possible to draw boundaries between his world and my world."[38]

The perspective of love is pre-eminently intersubjective. If we concentrate our attention on someone we love, "to exist no longer means '*to be there* or *to be elsewhere*'"—we are never far from someone we love. In fact, intersubjectivity, for Marcel, is love. The forms of intersubjectivity—friendship, marriage, paternity, fraternity—are all forms of love.[39]

Love should not be taken here in a sentimental or superficially romantic sense. Love "exhibits an incomparable dignity by which it transcends mere feeling."[40] Love is life which decentralizes itself, which changes its center. When we love, our interior defenses—self-consciousness, pretense—fall along with the barriers that separate us from another. Genuine individuality is a creation of love (intersubjectivity), because in love there is renewal and even rebirth. Someone who loves me "discovers me to myself." The "I" is a child of the "we." Marcel notes that the "I," "far from positing itself as essence, springs forth as lover."[41]

In Marcel's philosophy, the realization of the self is a gift of another, of many others. The rapport which is granted with another acts on us, not as an outside cause, but as an inward principle which develops us from within.[42] The other, for Marcel, is not a threat to our integrity, as in the philosophy of Sartre.[43] An attitude which posits an elemental conflict between ourselves and others is tense and suspicious. Since a conflict is always supported by our consciousness of it, its maintenance compels us to be constantly on our guard. We have to be always aware of ourselves, and of the distinction between "ours" and "theirs." An availability for communion is a relaxation in the presence of another, and an abandonment of tension. In an atmosphere of communion we are free to "be ourselves," just because we are freed of a vigilant consciousness of the self.[44] In Gallagher's words, "there is no self except insofar as there is communion. My self apart from other selves quite simply *is not*. It comes to be in communion."[45]

On October 24, 1922, Marcel notes in his diary a "feeling of inner indigence that I am experiencing so clearly." He says that "at these moments being reaches its lowest ebb." He observes that the ebbing of the sense of being seems to be bound up with the disappearance of the "thou"—other persons are treated as others, and the "I" (*moi*) sees himself as "him" (*lui*).[46] On the other hand, he sees that joy is bound up with a consciousness of being "all together," as when we take part in a chorus or a congregation. Joy is a consciousness our bodies have of their own functioning, when the energy of our bodies is synchronized with other energy (synergesis). Dancing is the obvious example: the joy of dancing is the harmony *we* achieve, the suppleness and grace which is ours, as our bodies move together with the music. Joy is an expansive mood; it leads us beyond ourselves in the direction of other being.[47]

We are most fully ourselves when we are most available for communion. Communion, or love, literally gives us our being, creates

> a reality at my deepest level more truly me than I am myself—love as the breaking of the tension between the self and the other, appears to me to be what one might call the essential ontological datum. I think, and I will say so by the way, that the science of ontology will not get out of the scholastic rut until it takes full cognisance of the fact that love comes first.[48]

IV. Participation in Being

To see the realization of our being in the communion of love gives us an important insight into what Marcel means by being. Any discussion of being in the context of Marcel's thought should begin with the admission that Marcel uses the word in different senses. As Marcel de Corte says, an ambiguity of this kind is one of the difficulties of an itinerant philosophy.[49] It is clear, however, that Marcel, throughout his writings, never considers being as a thing: "the expression of being as a noun (*l'expression l'être*) is itself detestable and empty of significance (*sens*)." To think being as a thing is to imagine "I do not know what level of resistance which subsists beneath the perishable bark of the phenomenon." The question of being, from this perspective, becomes a search for the categories which are adequate to describe an ultimate material. To initiate such a search is inevitably, as Kant saw, to transport "into the domain of metaphysics relations which are thinkable only between phenomena." Where do we stand to describe this thing which is called being? An authentic search (*quête*) into the significance of being, according to Marcel, would look for ways in which our own being reaches a certain level of liveliness or enhancement: " a mode of experience or life upon which the critical experience would no longer have any hold." This would not be an inquiry into being in a substantival sense—of *a* being or *some* being (*l'être*)—but of being in the verbal sense of what it means for us to be (*d'être*). This sort of inquiry into being can be intelligible, because it moves on the level of the phenomena, searching for what constitutes the fullness of human being.[50]

Marcel often says that the distinction between the full and the empty is "infinitely more essential," or more fundamental, than that between the one and the many. We know the sorts of experiences which bring fulfillment to our being: happiness, love, inspiration, joy . . . "There is being as soon as there is enjoyment (*jouissance*)." Enjoyment in this context does not mean a gratification which dulls our sensitivity into stupor, but rather a pleasurable participation in the joy which enlivens and enhances our being. Joy, Marcel writes, is "not the mark but the upsurge of being." Joy is fullness (*plénitude*), and has about it a spiritual or religious value. There is nothing more destructive of spiritual development than ennui, which is the consciousness of time as empty, needing to be filled. Being *is,* from the moment when hope discovers it has neither been deceived nor disappointed. Being abounds with the fulfillment of an awaiting (*attente*) to which we have given ourselves over without qualifications. (This awaiting or expectation would not be the half-hearted waiting of a Vladimir or an Estragon, but rather an active waiting in which a man of faith places himself entirely at the disposal of his trust.) The fullness of our joy, essentially, is a feeling of *resource.*[51]

Joy can be expansive and can yield enjoyment, because it is bound up with the sense of being given an inexhaustible resource. Marcel identifies being with the "principle of inexhaustibility."[52] Thus the value which the upsurge of being lends to our lives withstands; it cannot be exhausted or reduced by critical analysis. Marcel writes of being as "what withstands—or would withstand—an exhaustive analysis bearing on the data of experience and aiming to reduce them step by step to elements increasingly devoid of intrinsic or significant value."[53]

The fullness of being is not quantitative, as a sum. In fullness of this sort there is something which cannot be pictured—although it can be said that this fullness contradicts the "hollowness of a functionalized world," and grants the fullness of time to a time grown stale. There is in us an ebb and flow of life which corresponds to the increase and decrease of our being. The ebbing of the sense of being can bring a mortal sadness (*la mortelle tristesse*), a disappearance of joy. The inflow of being brings fullness and fulfillment. "The experience of being is fulfillment (*accomplissement*)."[54]

The essential thing about fulfillment is its creativeness. The word *creation* carries a special import in Marcel's analyses. Phenomenologically, it is not necessary that creation produce anything; the essence of creation can never be located in the making of something outside ourselves. There is a kind of production (the assembly line) which is not creative, and which is even destructive of creativity; and there is a creation which bears forth no objects. We have all known persons who are by nature creators, but who never have any discernible product to display their creativity: persons whose presence is a radiance which makes us glad to be with them; or persons who "add a positive contribution to the invisible work which gives the human adventure the only meaning which can justify it."[55]

What is essential to creation is the attitude of active receptivity. This is the deeper reason why it is not meaningful to identify creation with a product which is external to ourselves. The self disappears in creation, and disappearing finds itself in the realm of being. Love introduces us to this realm where being and creation coincide, as well as does inspiration.[56]

There is a close connection between creation and availability. Creation is an opening of ourselves to the gift in any of its forms: insight, inspiration, revelation of presence or of truth. The fulfillment of human being lies in ecstasy, in the strong and basic sense of that word (being led beyond ourselves, having our center outside ourselves). Human being cannot be sought as a residue left over when we have stripped away whatever is inhuman or inhumane; it can only be accepted and appreciated, as a present or a discovery. In the last analysis, our being is a gift, a gift we cannot give ourselves. Marcel sees that the Christian language of grace is most adequate to say that our being is a present to us from another, the creation of another. We discover ourselves in our *human* being "in the gift and in creation in all its forms."[57]

The more our existence becomes inclusive, the less we are separated from our being, the more we are. "The more my existence takes on the character of including others, the narrower the gap which separates it from being; the more, in other words, I am."[58] The way of the fulfillment of our being passes through communion. Seymour Cain locates two "moments" of "ontological communion" in Marcel's thought: "opening up" (availability) and "entering in" (participation).[59] Communion is ontological, because it is a *participation* in which we touch the source of our being.

Participation is one of the more difficult notions in Marcel's philosophy. Much of Marcel's reflection upon participation in the *Metaphysical Journal* is obtuse and unsatisfactory. Marcel himself speaks of this reflection, noted down before the first War, as "confused and so clumsily carried out," and "interesting only because of the intention behind it and because of the underlying experience I have attempted to evoke."[60]

In the Gifford Lectures, he runs through a series of examples in order to evoke the experience ("experiences" would be better) which the word participation is intended to allude to. A cake is brought in and set before us. It is there for all to see, we can observe whether it is large or small. We gather around it, around a table on which it sits, and each of us claims his share. The cake is sliced up, and we eat it. The meaning of participation here is obvious: it means to physically take a part or to consume. In other cases, participation takes on a more subtle sense, as when we claim our share in a collection of paintings. There is no sense in which we can *consume* a work of art. We can enjoy it, admire its creativity—but only on the basis of our availability to the spirit of the painting. Participation, as an admiration, is a receptivity, as well as an activity. Of course, our paintings can be bought and sold, and our only reason for buying them may be to hang on to them until their market value has risen and we can make of them a handy profit. Here in this example we are still on the level of having: we can take our "share" in the pictures in financial measures. If we think of participation in a ceremony, for example, the meaning of participation as a having begins to be transcended. The value of a participation in a ceremony cannot be weighed in objective terms. Value in this case is the strength we are given as we are all together, sharing a single love or devotion. We find our own purpose supported, because we know it is turned in the same direction as the purpose of many others. Let us say that the ceremony is one of thanksgiving to God for the end of a war or a national disaster. Very little is objectively given to us in this case: the announcement of the time and date of the ceremony, of the church at which it is to take place. What if we are ill, though, and cannot be there? What if we do not even know the precise time and date? Still we can join our prayers to those of other worshippers, and we can share in the mood of thanksgiving. "What can it matter to God whether I am physically present or not in such and such a church?" The intent of the ceremony surpasses the circumstances of time and place of meeting. It is the act of thanksgiving which is important. This ceremony of thanksgiving, convoked at a certain time, is only one expression of an attitude of adoration which is open to us at any time. Marcel's imaginative variation of examples shows how participation admits of increasingly subtler (more "spiritualized") gradations of meaning.[61]

Roger Troisfontaines distinguishes in Marcel's philosophy two levels of the meaning of participation. These levels are expressed through a dialectic of three "moments" of human life. The first moment, he calls "the state of existence" or "primitive immediacy." At this "moment," man is immersed in a situation which he has not chosen, and cannot have reflected upon. His senses, or more fundamentally his birth, give him this situation (*être-au-monde*). The participation at this moment of human life is an "existential community." Community is imposed (or provided), and begins with the entrance of the infant into the family.[62]

The second "moment" of the dialectic is "objective communication." Communication between the self and beings and entities independent of the self replaces the pre-reflective immersion in life. This is what objectification means, the isolation of "objects" (as placed in front of us) from the given immediacy. Objectification makes science possible, but it risks destroying the native participation man initially enjoys. It depends upon man to maintain or abolish the bonds of participation originally given.[63]

The third "moment" of Troisfontaines's dialectic is "ontological communion." Communion re-establishes broken bonds, and creates a new participation, which is entered consciously and freely. Troisfontaines's privileged example of communion is the same as Marcel's : the second chapter of his second volume is entitled, "To Love is to Be." Being, according to Troisfontaines's interpretation of Marcel, is distinguished from existence by the choice of the person who recovers his involvement ("couplings") with the world, with himself, with others and with God. Human life is a call, an invitation to make the journey from existence to being. Troisfontaines admits that Marcel himself has never explicitly formulated this dialectic, but he thinks it offers an "outline" through which Marcel's thought can be systematized.[64]

A neat distinction between existence and being cannot, however, be supported with Marcel's own writings. Marcel will sometimes think of an "articulation" (*un joint*) between existence and being which coincides with the attainment of freedom or fullness in life.[65] Gallagher thinks Troisfontaines's distinction is tidy but inexact.[66] More profound than the distinction Troisfontaines draws between existence and being (which is really not essential to his thesis) is the analogy he points out between two levels of participation: sensation and communion.

> The sensory receptiveness of the existent submitted to the influences of a surrounding world already prefigures or preforms the availability requisite for personal being to insert itself into a spiritual universe.[67]

Marcel considers this analogy fundamental.[68] He would not, however, say what Merleau-Ponty does—that sensation is a communion—for while "sensation can only be thought of as a mode of participation," still "participation considerable exceeds the limits of sensation."[69] Communion is a development of the submerged and pre-reflective participation of sensation. It extends the bodily meaning (*sens*) of participation. Participation engages us at varying depths. "Participation cannot be separated up into detail, but that does not mean that all is given to me at once."[70] Participation is one activity, and bears in one direction, but it crosses thresholds of greater profundity. Through sensation, our bodies give us participation in the world. Incarnate life introduces us into the reaches of communion. And participation in the mystery of being is through communion. This is why it is no contradiction for Marcel to speak of incarnation as "the central given of metaphysics" and of love as "the essential ontological datum."[71] For there is in Marcel's thought one mystery, the mystery of being (of which the mystery of incarnation and the mystery of intersubjectivity are particular expressions), and there are thresholds across which we are admitted to mystery. (It is never a matter of admitting, but rather of being admitted to what is mysterious.) It is possible for us to *be* more or less fully, as we cross thresholds of participation, to share a communion more or less profound.[72]

The ebb and flow of the sense of being is bound up with the knowledge of presence and of communion. In the presence of the thou we know who we are and what is the true measure of our worth. The communion in which we enjoy the elemental intersubjectivity given us functions as the milieu in which the creation of our being occurs. Our being is fulfilled—joyous, vital, full—in the communion of love. "To love is to be." Communion gives us the meaning (*sens*) of human being. Our being is the gift of another, and of a grace which occurs to availability. For it is our availability which is our "opening" upon the fullness and resource of communion. Availability is for communion, and communion is the fulfillment of the promise concealed in the directionality of availability.

Joseph Chenu, writing on the theatre of Marcel, sees in Marcel's thought a single intent of availability, which enters into a participation in being (to be) through participation (communion) with beings.

> It is by becoming authentically a participating being that we attain and possess this metaphysical being which would otherwise be a groundless abstraction: I am in the measure I participate in being; to participate in being and to participate in other beings are only two aspects of the same fundamental operation, of the same opening, of the same conquest of availability.[73]

It is availability which leads us, as well, to a revelation of a more profound significance of communion. Ricoeur points out that Marcel uses the same word, participation, to speak of communion with the thou and with the absolute Thou; and the same word, presence, applies to both the friend and to God. "The first image," he writes, "the first approximation I have of the hold of being on me is the influx of being which friendship (*amitié*) arouses in the very heart of my existence. And the first outline of my own permeability to being is my availability for my friend."[74] Ricoeur is referring to Pietro Prini's description of Marcel's philosophy as an "analogy of presentiality": a "concrete analogy" between the "absolute Thou" and the "us." (In a foreword to Prini's work, Marcel approves this description.) Through a "deepening" and "interiorization" of communion—in such concrete forms as fidelity to, hope in, love for another—Marcel recognizes "a 'Presence' from which all other 'presences' draw their life and worth."[75]

The next chapter will be devoted to the development, in Marcel's thought, of this recognition.

[1]Bergson, *Two Sources,* pp. 30-36 and 266-268.

[2]*Presence and Immortality,* p. 239.

[3]*Sens* is a marvellously ambiguous word. In English, the sense of a direction taken (an attitude or orientation assumed) is not linguistically close to a meaning (a significance, a relevance, or an import) which is disclosed or remains hidden. The very ambiguity of the word *sens* keeps these varying connotations bound. A way is a direction we have chosen, and always is fraught with significance.

[4]Troisfontaines, *Existence,* I, 44.

[5]*Journal,* p. 163. Cf. Martin Heidegger, *Being and Time,* trans. by John Macquarrie and Edward Robinson (New York and Evanston: Harper & Row, Publishers, 1962), esp. pp. 65, 149-168 and 308.

[6]*Presence and Immortality,* p. 214.

[7]*Journal,* p. 163; and *Presence and Immortality,* pp. 88, 100, 109, 151, 212, and 237.

[8]Intersubjectivity, for Marcel, indicates "the realm of existence to which the preposition *with* properly applies," the realm of *Mitsein* or communion. (*Reflection and Mystery,* p. 221.)

[9]*Reflection and Mystery,* pp. 177-178 and 218-222.

[10]*Journal,* p. 146; and *Presence and Immortality,* p. 237.

[11]Again, Marcel's descriptive example carries more significance in French than in English; for in English the polite and endearing form of address has fallen into disuse. "Thou" is used only occasionally, and with diminishing frequency, in our prayers. The French say *tu* to children, pets, loved ones and to God.

[12]Gabriel Marcel, "Theism and Personal Relationship," *Cross Currents,* I, No. 1 (1950), 37.

[13]Roger Troisfontaines, S.J., *De l'Existence à Être: La Philosophie de Gabriel Marcel,* II, Bibliothèque de la Facultè de Philosophie et Lettres de Namur (2d. ed.; Louvain: Éditions Nauwelaerts, 1968; Paris: Béatrice-Nauwelaerts, 1968), p. 21.

[14]Hocking observes that Marcel is not "down on objects," only on the assumption that the object is the "exemplary case of being." (Hocking, "Marcel," p. 445.)

[15]*Homo Viator: Espérance,* p. 18.

[16]*Journal,* p. 303.

[17]*Faith and Reality,* pp. 56-57.

[18]Ricoeur, *Marcel,* p. 169.

[19]*Existentialism,* pp. 39-41.

[20]*Presence and Immortality,* pp. 236-238.

[21]*Ibid.*

[22]*Being and Having,* p. 69.

[23]*Position et Approches,* p. 83.

[24]*Ibid.,* pp. 80-82.

[25]Ricoeur, *Marcel,* p. 182.

[26]*Presence and Immortality,* pp. 153 and 175.

[27]Troisfontaines, *Existence,* II, 192.

[28]*Réflexion et Mystère,* pp. 223-224.

[29]"Ontologie," pp. 19.14-4 through 19.14-6.

[30] *Presence and Immortality,* pp. 214 and 241.

[31] *Creative Fidelity,* p. 15.

[32] Gabriel Marcel, *Le Quator en Fa Dièse* (Paris: Librairie Plon, 1925), V. vi.190.

[33] *Presence and Immortality,* pp. 200-201. The difference between Sartre and Marcel may be, after all, that Sartre cannot see that there are ties which are liberating and not at all constrictive of our freedom.

[34] *Journal,* pp. 173 and 303.

[35] *Faith and Reality,* pp. 16-19 and 30-31.

[36] Hocking, "Marcel," pp. 451 and 458.

[37] *Human Dignity,* pp. 50 and 65. Cf. *Faith and Reality,* pp. 1 and 17. Cf. also Heidegger, *Being and Time,* pp. 172 and 179.

[38] *Searchings,* p. 69.

[39] *Faith and Reality,* pp. 30-31 and 191. Cf. *Human Dignity,* p. 147.

[40] *Searchings,* p. 65.

[41] *Journal,* pp. 62, 147 and 221.

[42] *Existentialism,* p. 22.

[43] *Human Dignity,* p. 141.

[44] Cf. *Homo Viator: Hope,* pp. 204-212.

[45] Kenneth Gallagher, *The Philosophy of Gabriel Marcel,* Orestes Brownson Series on Contemporary Thought and Affairs, No. 4 (New York: Fordham University Press, 1962), p. 8.

[46] *Journal Métaphysique,* p. 279.

[47] *Faith and Reality,* pp. 133-135.

[48] *Being and Having,* p. 167.

[49] Marcel de Corte, *La Philosophie de Gabriel Marcel,* Cours et Documents de Philosophie (2d. ed.; Paris: Chez Pierre Téqui, n.d.), pp. 12-16.

[50] *Journal Métaphysique,* pp. 181 and 202-203. Cf. *Faith and Reality, pp. 40-41; Being and Having,* p. 139; and *Creative Fidelity,* p. 26.

[51] *Journal Métaphysique,* pp. 177-178, 202-203 and 230.

[52] *Being and Having,* p. 102.

[53] *Existentialism,* p. 14.

[54] *Foi et Réalité,* pp. 39-40 and 46-47.

[55] *Ibid.,* p. 47.

[56] *Being and Having,* pp. 132, 150 and 152.

[57] *Foi et Réalité,* p. 33; and Marcel, *Invocation,* pp. 70 and 75.

[58] *Foi et Réalité,* p. 35.

[59] Cain, *Marcel,* p. 70.

[60] *Human Dignity,* p. 27.

[61] *Reflection and Mystery,* pp. 137-140.

[62] Troisfontaines, *Existence,* I, 45-46.

[63] *Ibid.*

[64] *Ibid.*

[65] *Foi et Réalité,* pp. 23-31.

[66] Gallagher, *Marcel,* p. 59.

[67] Troisfontaines, *Existence,* I, 304.

[68] *Invocation,* p. 119.

[69] *Réflexion et Mystère,* p. 141.

[70] *Journal,* p. 158.

[71] See above, pp. 71 and 90.

[72] The metaphor of "thresholds" is my own—not Marcel's—but it seems to me to express the notion Marcel alludes to in *The Mystery of Being,* when he speaks of "levels" of the self—"modulations" or moods of existence: "varied tones or tonalities (*tons*) of existence" (a musical metaphor, which should be kept in mind alongside the spatial one I have suggested). (*Réflexion et Mystère,* p. 146.)

[73]Joseph Chenu, *Le Théâtre de Gabriel Marcel et sa Signification Métaphysique* (Paris: Aubier, Éditions Montaigne, 1948), p. 71.

[74]Ricoeur, *Marcel,* p. 178.

[75]Prini, *Méthodologie,* pp. 7 and 117-118.

CHAPTER FOUR
Communion and the Absolute Thou

I. The Elucidation of Givens Spiritual in their own Right

Marcel wrote in the Preface to the English edition of the *Metaphysical Journal* (1950) that the "central theme" of that work—and of his subsequent works, as well—is that "being cannot be indicated, it cannot be *shown;* it can only be alluded to, a little as some third person now disappeared is alluded to amongst friends who knew him formerly and keep his memory green."[1] Metaphysical discussion, Marcel notes, usually sets out from a symbol which is visual: "the symbol of an object which remains what it is, which does not change its nature when, without ceasing to regard it, we move farther away from it."[2] What is implicit in such an approach to ontology is the assumption that there is "a sort of optimum position from which we will get the best possible view of this object." Imagine that I am looking at a landscape with a friend of mine. He points to a mountain he sees on the horizon. I think that what he sees is not a mountain, at all, but a cloud, and I tell him so (my perspective is better than his, and I know more about the topography of the region). This kind of comparison, Marcel maintains, is impossible in metaphysical discussion—or at least impossible if metaphysical discussion bases itself on the dimension of mystery and presence, rather than on the objective dimension. Visual imagery is essentially spatial; it leads (or misleads) us to look for relations which are *visibly* discernible, and for a sort of knowing which is detached from involvement. But the kind of knowing on which metaphysics is founded is participatory knowledge—immediate, direct, existential, more like sex knowledge than knowlege of objects in space. Faith, for example, is an intensely personal drama which directs a person's life in a certain way, and involves him at the center of his being. I cannot take another's place of faith, without becoming who he is, because *he is not distinct* from his faith. Marcel writes:

> This applies equally to the instance of love: I cannot hope to see my friend's mistress through his eyes without *becoming* my friend, whereupon it becomes impossible for me to appreciate the woman in question otherwise than as he does.[3]

Marcel's own ontology begins with the nature of personality and the personal order, and seeks to discover here glimpses of a supra-personal fullness whose reaches are inexhaustible and mysterious.[4] This does not mean that he appeals to a species of Bergsonian intuition, as a kind of mystic intelligence. In fact, he distrusts the pretensions of such an appeal. It is to ordinary experience and the exploration of its depths that Marcel turns. He thinks that transcendence cannot mean the transcendence of experience. Beyond the limits of experience, there is nothing. Unless there exists the possibility of experiencing the transcendent, that word can have no meaning for us. Transcendence is immanent in experience.[5]

Thus Marcel approaches being or sacredness through the intimate human experiences he looks upon as "the privileged ground of the sacred."[6] Just as illuminated surfaces reveal a source of a light not directly visible to us, so intimacy (communion) reveals beyond itself a sacredness which, although immersed in mystery, appears to reflection as that power without which communion falters and perishes.[7]

To change the metaphor somewhat, I could say that Marcel discovers a sacred or sacramental Presence, residing in the depths of communion. The metaphor of depth is not just another metaphor, for Marcel, replaceable with any other—height, for instance. The images which the metaphor of height conveys are only spatial; its reference is to the dimension of extension. Thus height cannot carry us beyond the level of exteriority: the level of objectivity, problematic and physical space. A "God on high" is a kind of God-object or God-idol, the God whose "death" Nietzsche rightly proclaimed. The metaphor of depth, unlike height, indicates what Marcel calls "time's other dimension": inwardness, interiority, intimacy. Marcel quotes with approval a line from Hölderlin: "Near and hard to catch hold of is God."[8]

Of course, images of depth do have a spatial reference. For instance, we think of a deep or profound idea, Marcel points out, as in touch with a region beyond itself, a region "whose whole vastness is more than the eye can grasp." There is the feeling that a promise is being made us, but we can catch no more than a glimpse of what its fulfillment would look like. But the distance of depth is not felt to be somewhere else; it is felt as intimately near to us, like a nostalgia for a homeland which is far away, but with which ties cannot be broken. It is as if this distance were somehow in our blood. The distance of depth, at the same time as it evokes spatial images, evokes images which are temporal. The deep thought or the profound notion is one which opens up before us a way which can only be followed in time. The deep thought "is like an intuitive dive into an investigation which can be developed only over a long period of time." But the notion of depth cannot be thought as futurity only; and futurity cannot, in this case, be taken as bare novelty. Marcel observes that we do not feel we are moving into depth, as we move into the future, just because we are experiencing novelty. It is not the novelty of the future which gives it depth. I could say that a temporal profundity requires the fidelity of the future to the past. Marcel says that the dimension of depth is a region where "now" and "then" tend to merge, and that such a dimension could be nothing other than Eternity.[9]

It is intimacy which puts us "in touch" with this region of the eternal deep (*tiefe Ewigkeit*), "time's other dimension." There is no authentic depth where there is no communion. Marcel says that the dimension of depth gives us "what is most intimate and most sacred in the human condition."[10] A communion which is profound includes the broadening dimension of distance. "There is a stifling intimacy which prevents the soul not only from opening out, but from breathing." This sort of intimacy could not be called profound; it is shallow, it has no depth and therefore no *Lebensraum,* no distance. A legitimate intimacy not only includes distance, but demands it. The metaphor of depth is irreplaceable to an authentic metaphysical inquiry, because depth invokes both the sense of the very close (*fascinans*) and that of the very distant (*tremendum*).[11]

Marcel's approach to metaphysical discussion moves through "the elucidation of certain givens which are spiritual in their own right (*l'élucidation de certaines données proprement spirituelles*)."[12] Paul Ricoeur writes that the originality of Marcel's concrete analyses, which date from 1929, is to link "the meditation on the absolute Thou" to concrete experiences, "at once recognized by all and incapable of stabilizing themselves without an act of transcendence which renders them spiritually possible."[13] Ricoeur is referring to Marcel's reflections on the human experiences of love, fidelity and hope, experiences Marcel considers intrinsically and ontologically profound. By penetrating deeply into such experiences, Marcel makes a "concrete" approach to the ontological mystery. His analysis uncovers the sense in which the absolute Thou resides in the human experience of communion.[14]

In the remainder of this chapter, I will look at the link (or bond) Marcel discovers between the thou and the absolute Thou—the Presence which Marcel thinks lies concealed in the heart of such specific ways of communion as love, hope and fidelity.

II. Love

Much of Marcel's analysis of communion and intersubjectivity applies also to the phenomenon of love, since, for Marcel, love is the paradigm of communion. Kenneth Gallagher comments:

> More and more Marcel approaches the position that any experience which opens us to another can be called love, until in the end we may not only say that communion is founded on love, but that communion *is* love.[15]

It is love which opens us to the other as other, and opens us to the Thou Who meets us as only . . . *Thou.* Love opens us to the infinite upon which it bears. Love reveals "a reality at my deepest level more truly me than I am myself." Thus Marcel considers love "the essential ontological datum," the starting point for his "concrete approach" to the ontological mystery.[16]

His consideration of love begins with a line which he quotes from one of his plays. One of Marcel's characters says, "To say that one loves a being means, 'Thou, at least, thou shalt not die.'"[17] The awareness of death as a problem is implicit in the act of love. It is, most of the time, not difficult for us to imagine our own death. Marcel writes: "As a rule, nothing is easier at a certain time of life than to accept death for oneself if one considers it a dreamless sleep without awakening; what cannot be accepted is the death of the beloved one, more deeply still the death of love itself."[18] It is inconceivable that there should not be in those we love some value more durable than the death which threatens to annihilate it. Someone whom we love, we acknowledge as presence and affirm as being. Unless we posit a radical separation of being and value, we must know that the *being* of the loved one is as perennial as his value. The affirmation of someone we love, in the meaning he holds for our love, carries with it a negation of the power of death. "Because I love you, because I affirm you as being, there is something in you which can bridge the abyss that I vaguely call 'Death.'"[19]

A love which is genuine, which is *true,* will not include the imagination of the death of the person who is loved. Marcel discovers at the root of love a primitive faith, a belief in "the inexhaustible richness and the unpredictable spontaneity" of "the beloved."[20] Love recognizes a promise of eternity concealed in its acts and affirmations. The language we use to pledge our love reveals our assurance of the promise: "Whatever changes may intervene in what I see before me, you and I will persist as one."[21]

Love wills the beloved as transcending death. The transcendence which Marcel means is not that of an eternal essence, and not that of an image preserved in memory or in a photograph. It is the *survival* of death which love affirms. Love, of course, does not create survival, but it does involve its affirmation. The notion of "survival" Marcel employs is ambiguous and unclarified. He does not want it to be taken as an objective fact, because as soon as it is taken in this sense, it becomes a figment of the imagination, and is thus of no ontological worth.[22] And he does not want survival to be understood as a continuation of life as such. The notion of continuation is itself an ambiguous one. "Experience shows us that certain creatures—I do not want to use the word 'beings'—are subject to what are real metamorphoses." The continuation of life through metamorphosis is not a survival in the human sense, since what is essential to our faith in the survival of someone we love is the perenniality, the integrity, beyond death, of the identity of the beloved.[23]

Marcel faces honestly the possibility that what he puts forward as a fundamental phenomenological insight into the inner logic and integrity of love may have "too subjectivistic a tone." "The emphasis," he writes, "is placed on the affirmation itself or on the assertion itself as such, and not on the thing which is affirmed."[24] The crucial point of his inquiry into the nature of love, however, is that, whenever an affirmation about another becomes love, it resigns all subjective claims in favor of the substantial worth of what it affirms. Love is precisely "the active refusal to treat itself as subjective." From the point of view of someone who has never known or given love—or from the point of view of someone who only "looks on" as spectator to *my* love—this affirmation which love contains must always appear monstrous and ridiculous. But the point of Marcel's approach is that certain concrete human phenomena, (fidelity, hope and love) can only be comprehended when they are accepted as privileged experiences for the understanding of human being.[25] Sam Keen writes of Marcel's phenomenological approach:

> The case for ontology rests upon a defense of the integrity of the logic and insight which is interior to the experience of love and the other concrete approaches from which it is inseparable. If one imposes upon love, faith and hope [an alien logic . . . the perspective of the spectator] and rejects them as subjective illusions, there can be no affirmation of being.[26]

Marcel wonders what sustains our belief in the abidingness of our love—and of the ones we love. The question turns upon our knowing whether the inevitable erosions of time and death can ever destroy that by which this being we love is truly a being.[27] Consider the value of the ones we love. We cannot imagine that this value will ever be lost to us. Nor can we imagine that the bonds linking our lives to our loved ones will ever dissolve. If death is final, then the value love discovers is destined to be lost. We have been deceived about the nature of what we thought would endure. Our love becomes a lie, and life itself a scandal. To admit that death is the ultimate scandal cannot be the same thing as to accept death as a fact of human experience, for this side of death nothing factual can be said about the ultimate reaity of death. We may have seen the *dying* of another, but none of us has experienced his own death. Acceptance of death as the last word on our love only strikes at the heart of those spiritual bonds (of communion) which form the condition of possibility of all forms of love.[28]

Marcel writes that love "implies the assurance: 'Thou wilt not disappoint us.'"[29] Love has no future, it can develop no trust, if it establishes itself on an anticipated disappointment. The assurance that our love has a future—and that the value of what we love in those we love will not be wasted—arises with a faith in the "Thou" Who allies Himself absolutely with our love. The spiritual dimension in which love resides, according to Marcel, is the same as that of faith. He writes:

> However strange it may seem to our minds, it is possible for there to be an unconditional love of creature for creature—a gift which will not be revoked. . . love is faith itself, an invincible assurance based on Being itself. It is here and here alone that we reach not only an unconditioned fact but a rational unconditional as well; namely that of the absolute Thou, that which is expressed in the *Fiat voluntas tua* of the Lord's Prayer.[30]

"To love someone truly," Marcel noted in his Journal, "is to love him in God."[31] As God offers Himself to our love, He confirms its promise and perenniality. This is true not only of the love between husbands and wives, but of friendships and family relations as well.[32] Marcel writes that solidity and consistency can be guaranteed (and expected) of the family's relationships, only if they have reference to an order beyond the human, whose sacredness is given us only through signs (*indices*).

> A family is not created or maintained as an entity, without the exercise of a fundamental generosity whose rightly metaphysical principle must be examined. We must, of course, leave on one side the man who generates by chance, who produces his offspring like the animals without accepting the consequences of his act. He does not found a family; he produces a brood.[33]

It is essential to love that it be open to the promise of eternity, and that it express that liberal graciousness or generosity which is one of the indices of sacredness.

Human love *is not*, unless it is "charged with infinite possibilities." If human love turns inward upon the self, it sinks into what Marcel calls "a mutually shared narcissism" and into an "idolatry," as well. But as love opens onto the presence of the thou, it includes the more profound openness to the Thou in Whom love abides and endures. (This is another of the places where Marcel finds "inexhaustible fertility" in the Bergsonnian distinction between the open and the closed.) The more absolutely we address another being as thou, the more we will be available to an absolute Thou Who offers Himself to love. The more we are available to this Presence, the more will the indestructible value of the bonds which have created "us" be assured.[34]

III. Hope

In his "Sketch of a Phenomenology and a Metaphysic of Hope"—a lecture given to the *Scholasticat de Fourvière*—Marcel begins the analysis of the experience of hope with an "I hope" of a very low order: "I *hope that* James will arrive in time for lunch tomorrow and not just in the afternoon." Two elements are implied here: a wish, and a certain belief. This is, as Marcel puts it, "a practical little problem of probabilities." I believe, with whatever measure of probability, that I shall attain the object of my wishing. My reasons for "hoping" in this case lie outside myself. There is nothing here for me to "take to heart." After all, it is a matter of no great importance whether James arrives at 1:00 or 5:00 tomorrow afternoon.[35]

When I "hope *that*," I always imagine the satisfaction or pleasure that would accrue to me if my wish were realized.[36] "Hoping *that*," essentially, is of the order of desire. In his William James Lectures, Marcel said that his reflections on hope during the Second World War had as their point of departure the criticism of Spinoza's identification of desire with hope.[37] Spinoza had correlated *spes* (hope) with *metus* (fear). Marcel wants to show it is desire, not hope, which is the negative correlate of fear.

> The correlative of hope is not fear, far from it, but the act of making the worst of things, a sort of pessimistic fatalism which assumes the impotence of reality or which will not grant that it can take account of something even if it is not just our good, but rather, as we think, a good in the absolute sense of the word.[38]

Desire tends toward possession; it has the thrust of "assimilating by destroying or consuming." Desire is "an anticipated appropriation together with the consciousness of a need hitherto unsuspected and even nonexistent, which this appropriation ought to fill." The appetite of desire is "rapacious."[39] The center of desire is within myself. The other, who is considered in desire, is considered only in reference to the enjoyments he can procure me, or the services he will be able to render me.[40]

Hope cannot be reduced to a desiring or to a kind of wishful thinking. Hope inevitably transcends the particular objects to which it seems, at first, attached. Locating itself on another level from that of ego-centricity, hope takes up what Marcel calls "an ontological position." I hope in a future whose arrival does not depend on me, and I do not lay down conditions to the fulfillment of hope. For this reason, hope is beyond the reach of disappointment. The more hope refuses the temptation to imagine "what I hope *for*," the more the distinction between hope and desire holds true.

> I take the example . . . of the patriot who refuses to despair of the liberation of his native land which is provisionally conquered. In what or in whom does he place his hope? Does he not conditionalise his hope in the way which just now we decided was unwarrantable? Even if he recognizes that there is no chance that he will himself witness the hoped-for liberation, he carries beyond his own existence the fulfillment of his desires, he refuses with all his being to admit that the darkness which has fallen upon his country can be enduring, he affirms that it is only an eclipse.[41]

Just as hope transcends desire, so it also transcends optimism. Marcel writes that the difference between hope and optimism "may seem to be more of a musical than a logical order." He may mean that hope has another way of dwelling in the world —another mood—than optimism.[42] The optimist looks at life as something outside himself, and considers the fullness of life as always beyond the horizon. He looks on his experience *"from a sufficient distance* to allow certain contradictions to become alternated or fused into a general harmony." His supposed reconciliation of opposites and conflicts depends upon a God-like perspective: across broad expanses and far into time. "If only we do not allow ourselves to stop too soon." The optimist is a spectator, while the man of hope is a participator. He engages himself in a creative process, entrusts himself to its development and assents to it from within. Marcel writes that this hope is a faith, and that it finds itself involved in a mystery, not face to face with a problem.[43]

Hope, since it ventures into the depths of the mysterious, is always more modest than optimism. The profound reason why we say that optimism is shallow is that it remains on the level of theodicy, rational argumentation and vague sentimentality. The optimist sometimes claims to found his beliefs upon practical experience, but the experience upon which he relies, Marcel thinks, is "not drawn from the most intimate and living part of himself."

> It is by no means certain that optimism does not always suppose the same disposition [*un même disposition*], the same *habitus*. Perhaps, there is no such thing as a profound optimism. The metaphysics of Leibnitz is certainly profound, but only so far as it is not optimistic and is not presented as theodicy.[44]

Marcel writes that optimism does not reach beyond the "I myself" (*moi je*). The optimist presents *himself* as someone gifted with especially penetrating vision. "If your vision is as good as mine, you cannot fail to see. . . ." His viewpoint is superior. "As your eyes are not as good as mine, do not hesitate to trust my testimony and my clearsightedness (Marcel's French is *clairvoyance*)." "To hope" can never mean "to flatter ourselves" so; the essential humility of hope will not allow such pretensions.

> "I hope [*j'espère*]" can never mean: "I am in on the secrets, the counsel of God, or of the gods, while you are a profane outsider. It is because I enjoy a special enlightenment [*ces lumières particulières*] that I affirm . . ."[45]

The threshold to genuine hope, in Marcel's analyses, far from being a special revelation, is the experience of despair. The example from which Marcel, during World War II, elaborated a phenomenology of hope was the situation of the prisoners of concentration camps, who endured waiting for nearly five years for liberation. Undoubtedly, many of these prisoners never expected to be released. They may have thought to themselves: "There is no reason for this war to end. I may die before the end. Better to risk everything for everything than to be stuck in this indefinite waiting." Impatience sometimes expressed itself in attempts at escape, which were rarely anything other than suicide attempts. The world of these men was bounded on all sides by inhumanity and hostility. There were some who could no longer "hold up" (who no longer bathed, shaved . . .), who capitulated to their imprisonment. This capitulation, on the level of personal relations, meant a failure of communion, as well as an impoverishment of communication (swearing, sarcasm, obscenity). There were, on the other hand, some prisoners who were inhabited by hope, who awaited the outcome of their imprisonment in confidence and trust. These prisoners remained open to the promise of their future and to one another: "a real communion was established among them." Around this community of the hopeful the cultural life of the camps (lectures, theatrical productions, religious services . . .) formed.

> It is absolutely certain that if those prisoners had been hypnotized by the long duration of their captivity, they would not have known how to profit from the time which had been turned over to them and which consequently would have remained a dead time, let us say even a *time of death,* for each individual would have been literally decomposed into impotence and depression.[46]

Marcel takes this condition of the prisoners as a symbol of the human condition in general. He sees an aspect according to which the lives of us all are a captivity, subject to depression and despair. This is particularly true of "contemporary man" and of man in the big cities, who is "as it were beleagured by despair." "I would go so far as to say that the great inhuman structures which close off the horizon on all sides are like the materialization of that temptation (to despair) from which it apparently grows more and more impossible to escape."[47] The simple fact that we are all born (and borne) unto death is enough to liken the condition of every man to that of the prisoner. The death sentence hangs over every one of us: death is a dire certainty for each of us. The limits to our life—limits which are co-natural with bodily existence—close in, imperceptibly, upon us, as if they were the confining walls of a prison yard.[48]

The human condition, so far as it is lived as a captivity, permits, even invites, despair. What is essential about this despair, according to Marcel, is the experience of closing, or of time as "plugged up."

> The man who despairs is the one whose situation appears to be without exit. . . . It is really as if the despairer kept hitting against a wall, the wall being faceless certainty, and yet hostile, and the result of this shock or impact is that his very being starts to disintegrate or, if you like, to give up.[49]

In despair, life is lived as "just one damn thing after another." "And there is nothing new under the sun"—forever and ever, Amen. Despair usually involves a ritualization of staleness. The despairing man re-enacts, in "dismal repetition, the eternalization of a situation in which he is caught like a ship in a sea of ice."[50]

Hope appears to despair as the act by which its temptation to capitulate, to be persuaded by the counsel of despair, is actively overcome. Marcel even writes that "there can strictly speaking be no hope except when the temptation to despair exists." The victory which hope gains over despair consists in its refusal to live a time grown tired with repetition. Marcel connects the attitude of despair with a certain perspective on time which he considers, not as an authentic empiricism, but as a dogmatism or a tyranny of the established. Such a view supposes "that time will bring nothing new beyond an illustration or added confirmation" of what we have already seen. If we accept the perspective of established experience, we find ourselves living "in a world where time no longer passes, or, which comes to the same thing, where time merely passes without bringing anything, empty of any material which could serve to establish a new truth or a new being."[51]

Hope, "with scandalously carefree grace," actively transcends that attitude, the precursor of hopelessness, which asserts: "It has never been found that . . ." or "It has never been seen that . . ."

> Hope is linked to a certain candour, a certain virginity untouched by experience. It belongs to those who have not been hardened by life. . . . In the name of accepted

experience people claim to trace some kind of circle of Popilius round us; "There is no way out"—that is the formula to which the experts of established experience fly. But postulated at the very basis of hope is the non-validity of such assertions, the truth that the more the real is real the less does it lend itself to a calculation of possibilities on the basis of accepted experience.[52]

Hope is "a kind of radical refusal to calculate possibilities."[53] Hope keeps its horizons open, and stays available to presences. Hope does not base itself upon established experience, but "is engaged in the weaving of experience now in process, or in other words in an adventure now going forward." If despair is the sense of time as *closed,* "hope appears as piercing through time." It is, in Marcel's words, "the prophetic character of hope" that allows something to pass through time: some good news or some new being. This is not to say that hope creates novelty. The nature of hope is that of an appeal, or an availability in a certain direction or dimension.[54] Hope "locates itself in a dimension which is that of perpetual novelty."[55]

Hope's refusal of the time of despair is a kind of non-acceptance which is positive and which Marcel therefore distinguishes from revolt. A non-acceptance can be a stiffening or contraction. When we tighten ourselves for resistance, we lose touch with our native powers and strengths. But hope incorporates the secret of relaxation into its refusal. Marcel compares this relaxation with "the supple movements of the swimmer or the practised skier." The difficulty for conception here is how there can be suppleness and grace in what appears to be a negation. Marcel shows the way out of this difficulty through the realization that, on whatever physical or spiritual level, stiffening or tightening up always reveals the presence of an attitude which, if it is not fear, is at least a concentration on the self. The essence of this concentration on the self, Marcel says, is "probably a certain impatience." The notion of patience brings Marcel's analysis closer to the character of hope. Take the expression, "to take your time," as an example. Someone who stiffens and tenses against . . . doesn't know how to take his time. A tennis instructor might say to one of his students who is obviously impatient and is forcing his shots: "Take your time." He means: "Do not force your own personal rhythm. Wait for opportunities to use the moves and skills which are peculiarly yours."[56]

Hope is patient with the self and "takes its time." Someone who faces a trial or test *with hope,* faces it with patience and relaxation. He considers the test as "an integral part of himself," and as "destined to be absorbed and transmuted by the inner workings of a certain creative process." So he does not contract; he relaxes in his hope. There is a "secret affinity between hope and relaxation."[57]

Hope is able to be patient with the other, as well as with the self. It never tries to do violence to the rhythm of another. Remembering that the other has his own autonomous rhythm, it never tries to "force" or "hustle" the other, substituting "my" time for "his." This patience implies a "pluralization of the self in time": a respect for the time the other needs to preserve his vital balance; and a placing of confidence in the time in which "we" grow and develop together. This means not only an acceptance of a temporal process as creative, but an embrace of the process, so that we promote it from within.

> It seems, strangely enough, that in hoping, I develop in connection with the event, and perhaps above all through what it makes of me, a type of relationship, a kind of intimacy comparable to that which I have with the other person when I am patient with him. Perhaps we might go so far as to speak here of a certain *domesticating* of circumstances, which might otherwise, if we allowed them to get the better of us, frighten us into accepting them as a *fatum*.[58]

Marcel clarifies the positive direction of hope through a consideration of hope as a *trust*. We hope that someone we care for will recover from illness, we hope for the return of someone who is absent from us, or for the return of peace to our land. In every case, we invest our hope in a future which does not depend on us; we hope for what lies outside the region of our possible independent action. To hope is always to lend trust, to place our confidence beyond ourselves. Hope implies the notion of credit, which I have already examined as the root metaphor of the Marcellian attitude of availability.[59] When I hope, I place myself in the position of someone who is asking for a grace (a gift). I am awaiting a favor or a generosity which I hope will be extended me. I assume that the mysterious source of generosity which I have "credited" with graciousness is neither insolvent nor indifferent to me.[60] I place myself at the disposal of this generosity, and I have confidence I will not be disappointed. Hope invariably expresses this confidence in the second person singular, in the language of intimacy: "I am sure that *you* will not betray (*que tu ne trahiras pas*) my hope." "One cannot have confidence except in a '*toi*,' in a reality which is capable of functioning as "*toi*," of being invoked, of being something to which one can have recourse."[61] Hope involves us in a *belief in* . . . . We can only extend "credit" to *some one,* to some power or presence, whether personal or supra-personal, capable of responding to our invocation in hope.[62] And our hope is most authentic when the source of our credit is inexhaustible, when our trust is accorded without reservations to a Thou Who is able absolutely to be a recourse for us. Marcel writes that

> hope consists in asserting that there is at the heart of being, beyond all data, beyond all inventories and all calculations, a mysterious principle which is in connivance with me, which cannot but will that which I will, if what I will deserves to be willed and is, in fact, willed by the whole of my being.[63]

Hope always has to do with "the restoration of a certain living order in its integrity."[64] When what I hope for is worth willing (for example, a safe journey for someone I love), it is impossible that I should be alone in my willing or my compassion. It is impossible that reality in its inward depths should be hostile or so much as indifferent to what I assert is in itself a good."[65]

At this point, Marcel's analysis of hope takes up a special difficulty: whether we can legitimately use the word "hope" to describe a situation in which "my own" existence is at stake. "When I tremble for my own existence, it may be that I am giving way to the simple instinct for self-preservation."[66] The case appears in a different light, however, when what Marcel calls "a piety to oneself" intervenes. He means by this "a reference to a certain spiritual interconnection at the heart of which my existence can preserve its meaning and value."

> We are not dealing here with an abstraction, an impersonal order: if I inspire another being with love which I value and to which I respond, that will be enough to create this spiritual interconnection. The fact of the reciprocal love, the communion, will be enough to bring about a deep transformation in the nature of the bond which unites me to myself. Where the matter concerns me alone, or more exactly when I consider myself as though I were the only one concerned, the question of knowing what is going to happen to me may strike me as practically without interest or importance.[67]

At the *Congrès Descartes* of 1937, Leon Brunschvicg, at the time France's leading proponent of critical idealism, accused Marcel of laying much more stress on his own death than he, Brunschvicg, was inclined to place on his. Marcel's response was that what is important in his eyes is not his own death, but the death of the one whom he loves. In a lecture given at a later time, Marcel adds that his own death is important to him only in consideration of the other, and the grief it would likely cause him.[68] When we know that someone we love depends upon us and is vitally affected by what happens to us, then we realize that a respect for another always involves us in a "piety towards ourselves." Thus our hope, in so far as it is a hope we hold in common, invariably transgresses the meaning of an organic attachment to ourselves. Hope resides in a dimension which is that of love—or communion.[69]

Marcel considers it essential to a phenomenology of hope not merely to discover the place where hope inserts itself into the world, but to search out the conditions under which it can find a sufficient response to nourish and nurture hope. He writes that if someone were to ask him, "Do you pretend that it is in my power to hope, although all the exits seem to be closed?"—he undoubtedly would reply:

> The simple fact that you ask me the question already constitutes a sort of first breach in your prison. In reality it is not simply a question you ask me; it is an appeal you address to me, and to which I can only respond by urging you not only to depend on me but also not to give up, not to let go, and, if only very humbly and feebly, to act as if this Hope lived in you, and that means before anything else to turn toward another—I will say, whoever he is—and thus to escape from that obsession which is destroying you.[70]

The pre-condition of hope is the availability which opens us to the other. Availability opens us to a "free field where hope can spread itself."[71]

Marcel's most formal statement about hope is that

> hope is essentially the availability of a soul intimately enough engaged in an experience of communion to accomplish—across the obstacles of willing and knowing—the

transcendent act, the affirmation of a living permanence [*pérennité*] of which this experience offers, at once, the promise and the first-fruits.[72]

The formula Marcel offers as the most adequate expression of the act of hope is: "I hope in thee for us (*j'espere en toi pour nous*)." This formula should be read in the light of one of Marcel's diary entries: in *Being and Having,* where he records the reflections upon which he develops his phenomenology of hope, he notes that hope is "a protestation inspired by love," and "a sort of call, too, a desperate appeal to an ally who is Himself also love."[73]

The "I hope in thee for us" has in mind a concrete event: the death of one who is loved. The "I hope" is located in the undying worth of the "thou" who is still loved through death. Hope here takes the form of a protest on behalf of the other—or even more than a protest, "a prophetic assurance." When two beings love one another, a living bond is created between them, an intersubjective unity, which is open in the direction of eternity and is "charged with infinite possibilities." This bond may be the relation between a man and a woman who have joined their lives in the sacrament of marriage; or it may be "a friendship, or *a fortiori,* a filial relationship, may also be the road which leads beyond the earthly horizon." The nature of this bond, when it is true, is such that its participants—the ones who share in it—cannot imagine its destructibility. The "prophetic assurance" against the death of the one who is loved, then, takes the form:

> Whatever changes may intervene in what I see before me, you and I will persist as one: the event that has occurred (death), and which belongs to the order of accident, cannot nullify the promise of eternity which is enclosed in our love, our mutual pledge.[74]

It is hardly conceivable that a holy God, Who offers Himself to love, should range Himself against that love, to deny or to annihilate it.[75]

It is in the light of the "prophetic assurance" of hope that Marcel's concept of the absolute Thou, Who offers Himself to hope, must be understood. The Thou (*Toi*) Whom reflection discovers in the act of hope is the "vital link" (*le lien vivant*) between the "you" (*toi*) and the "us" (*nous*).

> Thou [*Tu*] is in some manner the surety [*le garant*] of this union [*unité*] which links us together, me to myself, or one to another, or the "us" to the "others." More even than a surety which assures or confirms from outside a union already constituted: it is the very cement upon which it is founded [*le ciment même qui la fonde*].[76]

IV. Fidelity

Paul Ricoeur, in his book *Gabriel Marcel et Karl Jaspers,* writes that Marcel's phenomenological analysis of fidelity is "the blossoming of all the efforts of the *Metaphysical Journal* to know God as the Supreme Thou."[77] Marcel approaches the phenomenon of fidelity through the nature of commitment and of the pledge of ourselves which we offer when we make a promise to someone. The problem of commitment precedes that of fidelity, since we can be faithful only to commitments we have already given ourselves to. The problem which commitment raises, as Marcel observes in his philosophical journal, is: "How can I promise—how can I commit my future?" Marcel's type case, from which his reflections on commitment and fidelity develop, is a promise he makes to a sick friend to return to visit him: "I promised C_____ the other day that I would come back to the nursing home where he has been dying for weeks, and see him again." At the time he paid the initial visit, he came, perhaps, out of a sense of politeness. But while he was with C_____, he noticed how much pleasure his visit gave him. He was sorry for C_____, who is doomed to die, and knows that he will die. So he promised to come back again soon, even to visit regularly. At the time he promised, his commitment was unqualified. He *felt* the solitude of his friend and his suffering, and was moved to make his promise. He did not stop to consider that his feelings might change—as in fact they have. The pity he felt the other day is now no more than a theoretical pity: what "one" *ought* to feel in such circumstances. He admits that the feeling which bounded so spontaneously from him the other day is no longer there. A conflict has arisen: he has been invited to a play, and the performance takes place at precisely the same time as his sick friend is expecting a visit. If he were to go to C_____'s bedside unwillingly, he reflects, he would be unable to conceal his present mood. If C_____ knew what an irksome duty the fulfillment of the promise had become, he would certainly be more pained than pleased by the visit. "The truth is that in this situation there is something which does not depend on me; it does not rest with me to prefer the play to the visit."[78]

Marcel's example raises a host of difficult questions about the nature of commitment. Can we count on the disposition we have as we promise, that it will not alter later on? Can we swear that if our attitude does change, we will still act as if it had not? Would this not be to lie to ourselves, as well as to the person to whom we promise? How can we be sure that the surroundings in which we made the promise, and the conditions under which we promised, will remain constant? Perhaps, these conditions will so change that we will not be able to keep the promise. Isn't there something conditional about every committal we might make? Wouldn't we be more honest with ourselves and with others if, instead of promising, we said, "I can't promise anything, I'll do what I can, if I want . . . don't count on me . . ."? In short, where do we stand to make the sort of draft on the future that a promise of any kind assumes? Isn't a promise inevitably based on an inclination or situation which is entirely of the present?[79]

The position which Marcel describes as the "doctrine of the Instant"—represented by the André Gide of *Les Nourritures Terrestres*—would answer that all we can count on is "the fullness of the unclouded instant, savored in all its novelty." We have this present moment to enjoy. Life is a happening. The past is a dead memory, which can only weigh upon our freedom to live in the Now. The future binds us to a fulfillment we may never live to experience. We can only be true to the moment. So we identify ourselves with whatever state or mood we happen to be experiencing at this particular time—we deny the contribution of our past, and forbid ourselves any commitment to the future. Such a position, Marcel points out, is "not only a limiting position, but also a literary position"—much of the literature of our time depends upon it. "A man who really lived by it would be destined, is destined, and will be destined to the worst of spiritual catastrophies."[80]

It is difficult to see how human life could be lived with any humanness (or humaneness) in a world where promises cannot be made and kept, where denial and desertion become man's daily fare. Marcel quotes Nietzsche's statement that "man is the only being who makes promises." Of all the animals, man alone rises above time, as he is able to sustain relations of fidelity with his fellows. But if it is the lie—or even indifference—which lies at the center of our lives, there is no longer room left for integrity, the basis for trust has disappeared. As Marcel's drama so clearly shows, mistrust and betrayal corrode the foundations of human life. Marcel writes:

> As events have gone on showing for the last quarter of a century, wherever man betrays faith in man, wherever treason becomes a habit and then a rule, there can no longer be any room for anything but insanity and ruin. It can scarcely be different wherever the claim is made to establish a way of private life which disregards the vow of fidelity.[81]

Social and spiritual life are rendered impossible, when no one can any longer depend upon anyone else.[82]

But it is not only the making and keeping of promises, but the sanctity of promises which is the true requirement of humanness. Marcel shows that conditional promises—"I can't promise anything, I'll do what I can, if I want . . ."—are only possible in a world in which God is absent. "Unconditionality is the true sign of God's presence."[83] Every promise, whether this is recognized or not, relies upon an unconditional given. Implicit in promising is an intention to disregard certain variables of situation and emotion, which lie at the origin of committal. Promises conceal an unspoken affirmation about the future: "Whatever my state of mind, whatever happens, I have given my word . . . ." A promise asserts an identity of ourselves across time, as well as a sufficient reliability—even an indefectibility—in the situation of which we are part. If fidelity to a person is possible, either we assume responsibility for the inalterability in our feelings and in the situation, or else we recognize that "mysterious relation between grace and faith" which "exists wherever there is fidelity;" "And wherever a relation of this sort fails to appear, there is room for no more than a shadow of fidelity, a mere constraint imposed upon the soul, although it may be both culpable and full of lies."[84]

Of course, people do sometimes commit themselves "without reservations" on the basis of transitory feelings. But such promises are, Marcel writes, founded upon self-deception: "a kind of inner swindle." We cannot establish for ourselves any adequate ground of fidelity, because we can never be sure that our feelings are strong enough to resist the erosive effect of time and circumstance. Only a promise which embraces an invocation to the absolute Thou—"if I give way, if my heart sinks, if my strength fails me, do come and help me, do renew the fading life of my love"—reaches deeply enough into the power of being to confer the possibility of developing into fidelity.[85] A de-sacralization of human relations, while it does not mean the denial of any explicitly formulated promise, is yet "the drawing back by which a spiritual organism dwindles, shrivels, cuts itself off from the universal communion in which is found the nourishing principle of life and growth."[86] The foundations of fidelity lie established in a faith that promises, when they are true, are offered "before God." A private life which disregards these sacred foundations of fidelity invites decay and degradation to set in upon the tissue of intersubjectivity.

> The truth is that humanity is only truly human when it is upheld by the incorruptible foundations of consecration—without such foundations it decomposes and dies. Do not let us say, however, that it returns to nothingness. If this word has any meaning, which is not certain, it is on the level of reality far below the human structure. When man, by denying the existence of God, denies his own, the spiritual powers which are dissociated by his denial keep their primitive reality, but disunited and detached they can no longer do anything but drive the beings of flesh and soul back against each other in a despairing conflict—those beings which, had their union been safeguarded and preserved, would have gone forward towards eternal life.[87]

If the foundations of fidelity seem precarious, when they rely upon a conditional commitment, they seem, on the other hand, unshakeable when they are based "not to be sure on a distinct apprehension of God as someone other, but on a certain appeal delivered from the depths of my own insufficiency." We cannot "count on" ourselves, on our own resources, for the realization of fidelity. But such a "counting upon . . ." or "appealing to . . ." belongs, essentially, to fidelity.[88] In his journal, Marcel asks if we do not frequently live as if we were "in touch with" resources which are actually lacking in us. We live, as it were, "on credit" (again, he takes up this root metaphor of *disponibilité*). But if we live on credit, who extends us the credit? This problem of resource, or *resort,* consists in asking who gives us the courage (heart) to. . . .[89] Who gives us the unconditional assurance with which we promise? In fact, fidelity is only conceivable if, in the act in which we promise someone, we extend an infinite "credit" to One to Whom we *resort* for the assurance of our promise. Fidelity must spring from something absolutely given to us. As Marcel says: "From the very beginning there must be a sense of stewardship: something has been entrusted to us"—and as we are responsible to a "thou," we are also *responsive* to an absolute Thou Whom we depend upon for the faithfulness which we promise.[90] Responsi-bility which is true and trustworthy becomes a human possiblity when fidelity addresses an appeal to the absolute Thou Whom we cannot deny without denying the very fidelity His Presence confirms.[91]

The appeal which is at the heart of fidelity is a way of standing "before God" which Marcel considers in his descriptions of the oath (*le serment*) or the vow (*le voeu*). When we say to someone, "I wish for (*je fais des voeux*) the recovery of your wife or your children," we mean that this recovery would please us. We do not have to involve ourselves in such a wish. We can remain outside the situation of illness in which this man is sharing the suffering of his wife or children. The vow (*le voeu*), on the other hand, always engages us, so that it cannot be reduced to a simple wish or desire (*souhait*). A vow is an engagement which is pledged "before God," in the presence of a transcendent power. It invokes the Presence of the absolute Thou. Marcel distinguishes this situation of invocation from that of the *bargain,* which says: "If you will do me this favor, I promise in return to do this or that pleasing thing for you." The commitment made here is conditional. The vow is degraded, and has taken on the character of a bribe. Such a bribe, Marcel thinks, is quite impossible when a promise begins to play upon a register which is religious or sacramental.[92]

There is still something equivocal in the case in which we say we will respond gratefully to a favor (*faveur*), whenever we have received it. The visible expression of our gratitude (in words) will be the sign of the invisible consecration of ourselves to the power who has helped us. This consecration—which is of an *ex post facto* sort—says: "I will consecrate myself to you, only on the condition that you will show your benevolence to me." Or, "If you will reveal yourself to me through this favor, I will consecrate myself to you." An address of this sort still places us in the bargaining position.[93]

Marcel gives an example of the sort of prayer which expresses the spirit of the vow:

> "I ask you to reveal yourself [*te*] to me, to be present to me, so that I may consecrate myself to you [*toi*] in full understanding of what I do—because from where I now stand, I can only perceive you through the clouds of uncertainty which envelop me. I do not pretend that you [*tu*] should attach any value, for yourself, to this consecration; it will add nothing to who you are. But if you love me, if you consider me your son, it seems to me that you, not certainly for yourself, but for me, will want me to know and serve you [*te*], since if it is not given me to know and serve you, I am given over to ruin [*voué à la perdition*]."[94]

Such an appeal grasps the essential meaning of the vow, as Marcel perceives it. This appeal collaborates with a certain process of creation moving within us.[95] It implies no dogmatic notion of the power to which it is addressed. Marcel understands the sense in which the vow is creative (*le voeu créateur*) as analogous to the event of aesthetic creation. The novelist or the dramatist, when he creates, is seized by a reality given less to his glance than to "a sort of inward touch (*une sorte de toucher intérieur*)." This reality appears to the artist as independent of his personal will, and at the same time as subject to his creative impulse. Through him the power of creation passes into the world. (This is, at once, a paradox and a mystery.)[96]

The dynamics of the *vow* are the same as in the instance of artistic creation, in the measure in which the vow is *creative*. The engagement we make, when we swear fidelity to another, while it is a decision we make, is yet not simply an "I decide": "a transcendent is implicated, however indistinct my consciousness of it may be."

> The creative vow is nothing other than the *fiat* by which I decide [*je me décide*] to place all my energies at the service of this possibility, which already imposes on me—a reality which is still for me alone, but which demands that I transform it into a reality for all, an established work [*une oeuvre constituée*].[97]

The vow transcends the situation of independent volition (*le voeu, bien loin de se réduire à une simple velléitè*). It engages us in the presence of a transcendence, consecrating our promises, becoming the power of the fidelity we vow.[98]

In his Gifford Lectures, Marcel speaks of the oath (*le serment*) as "the word consecrating itself (*la parole se consacrante elle-même*)." And he points out that the word "consecrate" always has reference to the sacred.[99] "Fidelity," he says in another lecture, "cannot be separated from the idea of an oath." He means by this that the fidelity we swear to another invariably includes an at least implicit consciousness of the sacred. An oath is a promise which ultimately depends upon an absolute resource for its fulfillment.

> I make you the promise [*je m'engage envers toi*] that I will not abandon you. This engagement [*engagement*] is more sacred in my eyes the more freely I consent to it, and also the less your defenses against me, should I break it. I know, besides, from the very fact that I have bound myself so absolutely, that the means will undoubtedly be given me to keep my faith. This oath, although in origin and essence my act—or more profoundly, because it is my act—becomes the strongest bulwark of all the resources I can summon, against its loosening and dissolution.[100]

To swear fidelity to another means to commit ourselves absolutely: to enter upon the commitment with the whole self—or at least, to summon up that part of the self which could not be repudiated without repudiating the whole. It means to address our commitment to an absolute Presence, and to the integrity of being represented in this Presence. Marcel writes in his journal: "Across the attachments which the I vows to itself lies the shadow of another fidelity."[101]

Marcel locates two ways in which the absolute Thou is present to fidelity: in the "active recognition" of an ontological permanence; and through this recognition, in the reference to the Presence it indicates. In an undated entry. into his philosophical diary, Marcel notes:

> Being as the place of fidelity.
> How is it that this formula arising in my mind, at a given moment of time, has for me the inexhaustible inspiration of a musical theme?
> Access to ontology.
> Betrayal as evil in itself.[102]

In his William James Lectures, Marcel repeats the formula—"being as the place of fidelity"—and says that "one who is faithful would actually be on his way to being."[103]

Fidelity is only guaranteed its abidingness and value in the measure that it is *creative*—and its creative power is effective in proportion to its ontological worth. "Creative fidelity," in Marcel's writings, is a fidelity which creates the self.[104] The truest fidelity is creative. Marcel gives the example of the marriage whose union of the flesh is a sacramental bond and "the appearance of a new being in which the husband and wife fulfill and pass beyond themselves." Another example of a creative fidelity would be the family in which giving birth is a grace, an outpouring of a fundamental generosity, an availability to the creative spirit which passes through generations and which, like the flame of Lucretia, is rekindled with each new pro-creation. A creative fidelity renews the person who holds it, as it renews the person to whom it is given. "It is as though it had a chance—it is certain that there is nothing final here—to make him at long last pervious to the spirit which animates the inwardly consecrated soul. It is in this way that fidelity reveals its true nature, which is to be an evidence, a testimony."[105]

Creative fidelity is the testimony to an "ontological permanence" resident to its nature. This permanence which lives in fidelity is an abidingness which exists in time and which demands and implies a history. What abides in fidelity can only be alive in time. Permanence here clearly does not mean resistance to change and process; neither does it mean the permanence of a law, or the formal permanence of a pure validity. So little is fidelity directed to a principle, that it has a sacred duty to protest against any principle from which the life has withdrawn, any habit or interiority (attitude) become encrusted with the schlerosis of a sterile conservatism.[106]

The permanence fidelity recognizes is a permanence which appears as the active perpetuating of a witness, which appears *within* a fidelity which endures and by which we endure. Marcel gives the example of that Christian faith or faithfulness which stands at the origin of the Church. The Church is "an act of fidelity." The value of a witness (or testimony) is bound up with the fidelity which has become embodied in some body's life: whether the fidelity of a child to its parents, or of a believer to his *religio*. This value "lies in the faithful following, through darkness, of a light by which we have been guided and which is no longer visible to us."[107]

A witness to sacredness, or to value as such, is always sensual—"the senses are witnesses"—because the recognition which sustains witness depends upon the sensory nature of human being. "The ontological order can only be recognized personally by the whole of a being, involved in a drama which is his own, though it overflows him in all directions." The recognition is beyond the opposition of feeling and understanding; it is an *actual* recognition: as of Ulysses by Eumaeus, or of Christ on the road to Emmaus. "An ontology with this orientation," Marcel writes, is plainly open to a revelation, which, however, it could not of course either demand or presuppose or absorb, or even absolutely speaking understand, but the acceptance of which it can in some degree prepare for. To tell the truth, this ontology *may* only be capable of development *in fact* on a ground previously prepared by revelation. [108]

The active recognition of an ontological permanence given to fidelity means, Marcel points out, an abidingness of presence—or of "something which can be maintained within us and before us as a presence, but which, *ipso facto,* can just as well be ignored, forgotten and obliterated." Fidelity is an "active perpetuation of presence, the renewal of its benefits." Fidelity "prolongs presence" and corresponds to a hold which other being has upon us. [109] No commitment can be made just from "my" side: a commitment, and especially the engagement to which it leads, always implies the response of the other—and our response to him. Fidelity can only be shown to a person, never to a notion or ideal. When we speak of fidelity to an idea or principle, we are abstracting from what Marcel would like to call the "*preséntiel* context" of fidelity. A principle can make no demands upon us, and can be maintained in "presence" before us only as we sanction or proclaim it. [110]

Marcel distinguishes constancy from fidelity by revealing the *presence* which always lends itself to fidelity. We can be *constant* to an idea or ideal, or to a law. We can be constant in a perseverance towards a goal. But in such instances, the "sameness" of our purpose must be vigilantly and ceaselessly affirmed by an effort of the will, in opposition to a *staleness,* a rancidity which imposes upon us whenever we direct ourselves steadily enough toward a virtue or a goal. At the core of fidelity, on the other hand, lives a presence, a unique and novel *thou,* a friend. Fidelity to the friend can only be appreciated when it is pledged with an appreciable measure of spontaneity, in independence of a grudging will. We are constant *for ourselves*—we are faithful in our presence to the other, to thou. [111]

This is why Marcel writes that what he calls a "piety towards the dead" is a refusal to betray a person who has existed by treating him as if he no longer existed. "If you say 'they no longer exist' you are not only denying them, you are denying yourself and perhaps making an absolute denial." [112]

This is also why the "ontological permanence" evident to fidelity comes as a Presence. It is presence which abides. "An absolute fidelity involves an absolute person." A fidelity given, absolutely, to another acknowledges the Presence of One in Whose sight we bind ourselves—as in the sacrament of marriage. [113] A fidelity offered to a thou is an availability for the absolute Thou in Whom the abidingness of our promise is kept. Roger Troisfontaines observes that such availability is the essential aspect of fidelity. [114] Marcel writes, "Creative fidelity consists in maintaining ourselves actively in a state of permeability, and we see here a sort of mysterious exchange between the free act and the gift in response to it." [115]

[1] *Journal,* p. viii.

[2] *Ibid.,* p. 313.

[3] *Ibid.,* pp. 313-314. Cf. *Being and Having,* pp. 120-121.

[4] *Homo Viator: Hope,* p. 26.

[5] *Reflection and Mystery,* pp. 57-59. Cf. *Presence and Immortality,* pp. 125 and 135.

[6] Gabriel Marcel, "The Sacred in the Technological Age," *Theology Today,* XIX, No. 1 (1962), 37.

[7] "Ontologie," p. 19.14-15.

[8] *Reflection and Mystery,* pp. 237 and 242.

[9] *Ibid.,* pp. 236-239.

[10] *Mass Society,* pp. 266-267.

[11] Cf. *Homo Viator: Hope,* pp. 217 and 162.

[12] *Être et Avoir,* p. 173.

[13] Ricoeur, *Marcel,* p. 294.

[14] Cf. *Being and Having,* p. 103.

[15] Gallagher, *Marcel,* p. 78. Cf. *Faith and Reality,* pp. 30-31 and 191; and *Human Dignity,* p. 147. Cf. also above pp. 57-74.

[16] *Being and Having,* p. 167; and *Journal,* p. 158.

[17] *Faith and Reality,* p. 68.

[18] "Theism," p. 41.

[19] *Faith and Reality,* p. 69.

[20] *Fragments,* p. 109.

[21] *Ibid.,* pp. 172-173.

[22] *Ibid.,* pp. 97-98.

[23] *Faith and Reality,* pp. 68-69.

[24] *Ibid.,* p. 69.

[25] *Ibid.,* pp. 68-75.

[26] Sam Keen, *Gabriel Marcel,* Makers of Contemporary Theology, No. 6 (Richmond, Virginia: John Knox Press, 1967), p. 32. The insertion into the quote is my own, and is intended to paraphrase Keen.

[27] *Faith and Reality,* pp. 171-172.

[28] *Homo Viator: Hope,* p. 152. Cf. above, Chapter Three.

[29] "Theism," p. 41.

[30] *Creative Fidelity,* p. 136.

[31] *Journal,* p. 158.

[32] *Faith and Reality,* pp. 175-176.

[33] *Homo Viator: Hope,* pp. 84-97. Cf. *Homo Viator: Espérance,* p. 123.

[34] *Faith and Reality,* p. 175.

[35] *Homo Viator: Hope,* p. 29.

[36] *Ibid.,* pp. 44-45.

[37] *Human Dignity,* pp. 141-142.

[38] *Being and Having,* pp. 74-75.

[39] Gabriel Marcel, "Desire and Hope," in *Readings in Existential Phenomenology,* ed. by Nathaniel Lawrence and Daniel O'Connor (Englewood Cliffs, N.J.: Prentice-Hall, Inc., 1967), p. 279.

[40] *Presence and Immortality,* pp. 231-232.

[41] *Homo Viator: Hope,* pp. 32 and 44-48. Marcel says that hope resides in a zone which is also that of prayer. (*Being and Having*), p. 74.

[42] See above, pp. 85-87.

[43] *Homo Viator: Hope,* pp. 33-35. See above, pp. 47-48.

[44] *Homo Viator: Espérance,* p. 43.

[45] *Ibid.,* pp. 44-45.

[46] "Desire and Hope," pp. 280-282.

[47] *Ibid.*, p. 282.

[48] *Ibid.*, p. 281.

[49] *Ibid.*

[50] *Homo Viator: Hope*, p. 42.

[51] *Ibid.*, pp. 36 and 51-52.

[52] *Ibid.*, p. 51.

[53] *Being and Having*, p. 79.

[54] *Homo Viator: Hope*, pp. 52-53.

[55] "Desire and Hope," p. 278.

[56] *Homo Viator: Hope*, pp. 38-39.

[57] *Ibid.*, p. 39.

[58] *Ibid.*, pp. 39-40.

[59] See above, pp. 13-16.

[60] Marcel's metaphor of credit includes a double reference: to the credit I receive, in the sense of a grace; and to the "credit" I give, in the sense of my belief—credibility, or credit-ability.

[61] *Faith and Reality*, pp. 86-89. Cf. *Homo Viator: Hope*, pp. 41 and 55; *Being and Having*, pp. 74-75; and *Existentialism*, pp. 27-28.

[62] *Faith and Reality*, pp. 88-89.

[63] *Existentialism*, p. 28.

[64] *Being and Having*, p. 75.

[65] *Existentialism*, p. 28.

[66] *Homo Viator: Hope*, p. 49.

[67] *Ibid.*

[68] *Faith and Reality*, p. 169. "Desire and Hope," p. 284.

[69] *Homo Viator: Hope*, pp. 50 and 57.

[70] "Desire and Hope," p. 284.

[71] *Ibid.*, p. 284.

[72] *Homo Viator: Expérance*, p. 86.

[73] *Being and Having*, p. 79.

[74] *Faith and Reality*, pp. 171-174.

[75] *Ibid.*, pp. 174-175.

[76] *Homo Viator: Espérance*, p. 77.

[77] Ricoeur, *Marcel*, p. 294.

[78] *Creative Fidelity*, pp. 159-160. *Being and Having*, pp. 47-48.

[79] *Being and Having*, pp. 41, 43-44 and 50. *Creative Fidelity*, pp. 158-160.

[80] *Being and Having*, pp. 194-196. *Creative Fidelity*, pp. 160-162.

[81] *Homo Viator: Hope*, p. 96. *Being and Having*, p. 14.

[82] *Creative Fidelity*, p. 16.

[83] "Theism," p. 40.

[84] *Being and Having*, pp. 41-42 and 54.

[85] "Theism," p. 40.

[86] *Homo Viator: Hope*, p. 89.

[87] *Ibid.*, p. 96.

[88] *Creative Fidelity*, p. 167.

[89] *Presence and Immortality*, p. 123.

[90] *Being and Having*, pp. 14-15.

[91] Cf. *Being and Having*, p. 45.

[92] *Homo Viator: Espérance*, pp. 151-152.

[93] *Ibid.*, p. 152.

[94] *Ibid.*

[95] Cf. above, pp. 93-95.

[96] *Homo Viator: Espérance*, pp. 152-153.

[97] *Ibid.*, p. 153.

[98] *Ibid.*

[99] *Foi et Réalité,* p. 131.

[100] *Homo Viator: Espérance,* pp. 174-175.

[101] *Being and Having,* pp. 46 and 55.

[102] *Ibid.,* p. 41.

[103] *Human Dignity,* p. 66.

[104] *Being and Having,* p. 96.

[105] *Homo Viator: Hope,* pp. 86-95 and 134.

[106] *Existentialism,* pp. 35-36. *Being and Having,* pp. 96 and 120.

[107] *Existentialism,* pp. 97-98. *Being and Having,* pp. 96 and 120.

[108] *Being and Having,* pp. 96 and 120.

[109] *Existentialism,* pp. 35-36.

[110] *Being and Having,* pp. 46 and 96.

[111] *Creative Fidelity,* pp. 153-155.

[112] *Being and Having,* pp. 96-97.

[113] *Ibid.*

[114] Troisfontaines, *Existence,* I, p. 377.

[115] *Position et Approches,* pp. 80-81.

CONCLUSION

Merleau-Ponty writes that sensation, or our bodily attitude toward . . . , expresses our being-in-the-world in one of two fundamental *rhythms* of existence: "adduction" or "abduction." Both adduction and abduction are forms of existence in relation to the world around us—to objects and to presences. In adduction we are open to . . . , and in abduction we have turned away from . . . .[1] In psychological terms, instead of "rhythms" of existence, I could speak of adient or approach behavior (trust, liking, co-operation), and of abient or avoidance behavior (mistrust, fear, manipulation). As an attitude, the Marcellian phenomenon of availability can carry both the existential and the psychological meanings. Availability is a facing toward . . . ; unavailability is a turning of the face away from . . . .

The attitudinal difference between availability and unavailability is what is intended by the etymological sense of the word "conversion": a "turning around" to face and to walk in another direction. "Conversion" means a change of perspective which involves us at our most interior and personal level. It alters our perceptions, changes the world in which we live, and changes us as we live in the world. (As, for example, the mystic vision of God, considered not *of* God as spectacle, but rather the gift of vision from the perspective of God. The mystics may have seen another world, as they saw the world from this perspective.) A "conversion" from unavailability to availability gives us a radically new "vision" upon . . . , or a new vision into . . . .

The ellipses which leave the intentional "object" of availability (or of unavailability) unspecified are purposeful. For the directionality (the reach) of availability puts us ever more profoundly "in touch" with the world and with presences. It would be relevant here to recall the notion conveyed by the French *sens,* whose ambiguity, laden with possibility for phenomenological disclosure, I pointed to at the beginning of Chapter Three. *Sens,* I pointed out, can mean a direction taken, or an orientation assumed. It can also mean a relevance or import (a bearing upon . . .), a significance. The meaning of *sens,* as a significance, is never far from the image of a way chosen. The *sens* of availability indicates the significance, provisionary and eventual, which may be found along the way toward which the attitude turns us.

The first "sense" of availability lies in the meaning it has for the life of our bodies. The openness of the personal body is an initial availability. Every more profound reach into the directionality which availability offers is "grounded" in this initial availability. A kind of bodily awareness goes ahead of our reflected consciousness, so that with the advent of every act, every intent of consciousness, we find that our life, so far as it is incarnate life, is always already a life in the world (*être-au-monde*). The personal body is a gift of our incarnation, an availability given to each of us. Prior to any conscious choice, or any determination of attitude we might make, our bodies invite us to explore the given world—in the objective, *présentiel*, and sacral dimensions—upon which they open us. Our bodies give us a *Lebensraum*, room for living and room where we can be with the other in the enjoyment of communion. Our bodies give us a primordial space in which we can receive presents and welcome presence. Our bodies are our access—to distance and to deep intimacies.

A more profound "sense" of availability begins to be indicated, when it is seen as availability for communion. As Kenneth Gallagher said: "My presence to the world is *by* spatiality, but it is *for* communion."[2] Communion is the fulfillment of the promise hidden in the pre-reflective participation of (bodily) sensation. Communion is an entrance into the life of the other, of the *thou*, whose presence availability opens us upon.

The fullest and most profound meaning (*sens*) of availability is found in the revelation of Presence, absolutely: the Presence of the absolute Thou. The way into the Presence of the Thou leads through the deepening and interiorization of the forms of communion with the empirical thou.[3] Concrete experiences of human intersubjectivity—love, fidelity, hope—reveal in their depths an appeal to the absolute Thou without which no genuine intersubjectivity is conceivable.

The meaning of unavailability is not a *sens*. The most significant thing about unavailability is that it is lacking in depth or profundity. Unavailability goes no place, it takes us nowhere. It shuts us off from the world, encloses us in ourselves, so that its "reach" remains close, or even enclosed. Unavailability does not get us even so far as into the other, to share his world, his perspective and presence. Availability, on the other hand, reaches deeply and distantly—distantly into depth.

The theological and philosophical implications of availability are apparent. Availability, I said in the Introduction, is a "foundational" concept; it discloses what I would call the "attitudinal foundations" of religious life, and of authentic human being. In Chapter One, I tried to show the despairing consequences of the directionality (or lack of it) of unavailability. I could also speak of the "pathological" possibilities of unavailability, if the analogy with a sickness which has an organic basis is not taken too strictly. It would be better to speak of a manifested unavailability as a dis-ease, rather than as a disease—or as a mal-aise, rather than a malaise. The meaning of the mal-aise of unavailability is a *human* meaning, or an attitudinal one, which finds expression in the personal body, but whose genesis cannot be discovered in the objective body.

I examined the attitude of unavailability through its indices of encumbrance, crispation, susceptibility and moral ego-centricity. The indices to unavailability disclosed the connection of unavailability with pride, and with what the ancient Hebrews called a "hardening of the heart." A possible translation of the phenomenon of hardening of the heart might be a stiffening against . . . , or an assuming of a rigid attitude toward. . . . In body language, rigid posture and tensed muscles tell the world of our unavailability. (The personal body always appears as a translation of an attitude of *ourselves* into terms of flesh.) When the mal-aise of unavailability is seen as rooted in an attitude of *ourselves,* an understanding of how the mal-aise or despair is related to the fundamental choices life offers us is possible.

Also, in Chapter One I showed how, in Marcel's analyses, availability and the presence of the other are related to "self-presence." The alienated self is the self which is divided interiorly, or the self which is far from "the presence of the self to itself."[4] It is as we are open to the presence of another that we discover the sense of who we are when we are most present to ourselves. The way of availability is the way beyond alienation.

This insight of Chapter One is supported by Marcel's analysis of "creation," which I discussed in Chapters Three and Four.[5] The fullness of our *human* being comes to us in the gift which Marcel describes as *creative.* It is in the creation which happens to us, rather than in a production which issues from us that Marcel locates the essence of creation.[6] Creation is abundant with ontological possibility. It is the self we can be, the authentic or *true* being which is the promise of our existence, which is the gift of creation.

This is seen most clearly in the nature of fidelity as *creative.* Human life which can "count on" any measure of reliability, or which can incorporate any degree of trustfulness, depends upon the sanctity of promises. Promises which are kept enable trust. But broken promises implant mistrust and disappointment at the heart of human experience. When our anticipations are repeatedly disappointed, we hold ourselves back, we stiffen our muscles (ourselves) against. . . . Our life atrophies, shuts itself in upon itself in one of the forms of unavailability. To the contrary, when promises made to us have been kept, we are available in trust. We "have no reason to expect" that the promises of the future will not continue to be kept. When we are able to trust the matrices from which our lives emerge (as creative) and the others upon whom we depend (as intending the enhancement of our life) then we can abandon ourselves to the creative possibilities of our time, the opportunities for growth, health and fulfillment. A fidelity which is *creative,* is creative of the self. Without a minimal fidelity (the reliability of, at least, some promises), human life cannot be lived, humanly.

I spoke of the *sanctity* of promises. Interhuman or social integrity is enough to allow us a provisional trustfulness (openness, availability). But if the ultimate context of our lives is not trustworthy, then what we have provisionally accepted as integrity turns out to be deceit on a grand scale, and our trust falters. A life of trust is ultimately possible only as trust develops into faith, into an attitude toward an absolute Presence Whom we can address with the unrestricted assurance: "Thou wilt not disappoint us."[7] It is trust which constitutes the native openness of availability. Without trust we would recoil from the other, and withdraw from the world into the seclusions of unavailability. When trust becomes faith, the horizons of availability open upon infinity. The open attitude of availability becomes a cosmic openness, and as Bergson says, our bodies reach to the stars.[8] Marcel says that "an open or expectant state of mind" implies faith or is already faith.[9]

If it is availability which constitutes the attitudinal foundation of faith, then, in a sense, it is true for us to say: whether we can count on the Presence of God—or whether we must suffer from an absence or eclipse of God—depends upon our "atittude." Prini writes that

> the whole of [Marcel's] inquiry has been guided by this simple and profound concept: the *veiled presence* of being illumines us in our incarnation in the world and our participation in the life of others, if we are disposed to recognize it [*si nous nous disposons la reconnaître*], if we escape our opaque self-consciousness from which issue the tensions of concupiscence and the inertias of denial.[10]

As Marcel sees, it does not depend upon us to hope or to love. But it does depend on us to take a certain step—in one direction or another—or to make a certain gesture. A gift (grace) cannot be received by someone who does not make room in himself for it. A gift is an appeal *and* our response to it.[11]

[1]Merleau-Ponty, *Perception,* pp. 211-213.
[2]Gallagher, *Marcel,* p. 22.
[3]See above, pp. 104-109.
[4]See above, pp. 35-39.
[5]See above, pp. 90-103 and 143-147.
[6]See, for example, *Foi et Réalité,* pp. 39-40 and 46-47.
[7]See "Theism," p. 41.
[8]Bergson, *Two Sources,* p. 258.
[9]*Being and Having,* p. 202.
[10]Prini, *Méthodologie,* pp. 119-120.
[11]*Homo Viator: Hope,* pp. 62-63.

BIBLIOGRAPHY

Primary Works

Marcel, Gabriel. *Being and Having: An Existentialist Diary*. Translated by Katharine Farrer. Harper Torchbooks. New York: Harper & Row, Publishers, 1965.

_____. *Creative Fidelity*. Translated by Robert Rosthal. New York: The Noonday Press, a division of Farrar, Straus and Company, 1964.

_____. *Le Déclin de la Sagesse*. Paris: Librairie Plon, 1954.

_____. "Desire and Hope." *Readings in Existential Phenomenology*. Edited by Nathaniel Lawrence and Daniel O'Connor. Englewood Cliffs, New Jersey: Prentice-Hall, Inc., 1967.

_____. *Du Refus à l'Invocation*. Paris: Gallimard, 1940.

_____. *Être et Avoir*. Philosophie de l'Esprit. Paris: Ferdinand Aubier, Éditions Montaigne, 1935.

_____. *The Existential Background of Human Dignity*. Cambridge, Massachusetts: Harvard University Press, 1963.

_____. *Homo Viator: Introduction to a Metaphysic of Hope*. Translated by Emma Craufurd. Harper Torchbooks. 3d. ed. New York: Harper & Row, Publishers, 1965.

_____. *Homo Viator: Prolégomènes à une Métaphysique de l'Espérance*. Philosophie de l'Esprit. 2d. ed. Paris: Aubier, Éditions Montaigne, 1963.

_____. *Journal Métaphysique*. Bibliotèque des Idées. 11th ed. Paris: Librairie Gallimard, 1935.

_____. *Man against Mass Society*. Translated by G. S. Fraser. Chicago: Henry Regnery Company, 1962.

_____. *Metaphysical Journal*. Translated by Bernard Wall. Chicago: Henry Regnery Company, 1952.

_____. *Le Mystère de l'Être*. Vol. I: *Réflexion et Mystère*. Paris: Aubier, Éditions Montaigne, 1951.

_____. *Le Mystère de l'Être*. Vol. II: *Foi et Réalité*. Paris: Aubier, Éditions Montaigne, 1951.

_____. *The Mystery of Being*. Vol. I: *Reflection and Mystery*. Translated by G. S. Fraser. 5th ed. Chicago: Henry Regnery Company, 1969.

_____. *The Mystery of Being*. Vol. II: *Faith and Reality*. Translated by René Hague. 6th ed. Chicago: Henry Regnery Company, 1970.

_____. *Philosophical Fragments (1909-1914) and the Philosopher and Peace*. Translated by Viola Herms Drath. Notre Dame, Indiana: University of Notre Dame Press, 1965.

_____. *The Philosophy of Existentialism*. Translated by Manya Harari. 5th ed. New York: The Citadel Press, 1965.

_____. *Position et Approches Concrètes du Mystère Ontologique*. Philosophes Contemporains: Textes et Études. Louvain: Éditions Nauwelaerts, 1967. Paris: Béatrice-Nauwelaerts, 1967.

_____. *Presence and Immortality*. Translated by Michael A. Machado. Pittsburgh: Duquesne University Press, 1967.

_____. *Présence et Immortalité*. Homo Sapiens. Paris. Flammarion, Éditeur, 1959.

_____. *Problematic Man*. Translated by Brian Thompson. New York: Herder & Herder, 1967.

_____. "The Sacred in the Technological Age." *Theology Today*, Vol. XIX, No. 1 (1962), 27-38.

_____. *Searchings*. Edited by Wolfgang Ruf. New York: Newman Press, 1967.

_____. "Solipsism Surmounted." *Philosophy Today*, Vol. X, No. 314 (1966), 204-210.

_____. "Theism and Personal Relationship." *Cross Currents*, Vol. I, No. 1 (1950), 35-42.

_____. "Vers une Ontologie Concrete." *Encyclopedie Française*, Vol. XIX.

Secondary Works

Bertman, Martin A. "Gabriel Marcel on Hope." *Philosophy Today,* Vol. XIV, No. 214 (1970), 101-105.

Cain, Seymour. *Gabriel Marcel.* Studies in Modern European Literature and Thought. New York: Hillary House Publishers, Ltd., 1963.

_____. "Gabriel Marcel's Way." *The Commonweal,* Vol. LXXIII, No. 11 (1960), 271-274.

Chenu, Joseph. *Le Théâtre de Gabriel Marcel et sa Signification Métaphysique.* Paris: Aubier, Éditions Montaigne, 1948.

Collins, James. *The Existentialists: A Critical Study.* 5th ed. Chicago: Henry Regnery Company, 1964.

Corte, Marcel de. *La Philosophie de Gabriel Marcel.* Cours et Documents de Philosophie. 2d. ed. Paris: Chez Pierre Téqui, n. d.

Davy, Marie Magdeleine. *Un Philosophe Itinerant: Gabriel Marcel.* Homo Sapiens. Paris: Flammarion, Éditeur, 1959.

Gallagher, Kenneth T. *The Philosophy of Gabriel Marcel.* Orestes Brownson Series on Contemporary Thought and Affairs, No. 4. New York: Fordham University Press, 1962.

Gerber, Rudolph I. "Marcel and the Experiential Road to Metaphysics." *Philosophy Today,* Vol. XII, No. 4/4 (1968), 262-281.

_____. "Marcel's Phenomenology of the Human Body." *International Philosophical Quarterly,* Vol. IV, No. 3 (1964), 443-463.

Gilson, Étienne, ed. *Existentialisme Chrétien: Gabriel Marcel.* Présences. Paris: Librairie Plon, 1947.

Grimsley, Ronald. *Existentialist Thought.* 2d. ed. Cardiff, Wales: University of Wales Press, 1960.

Harper, Ralph. *Nostalgia: An Existential Exploration of Longing and Fulfillment in the Modern Age.* Cleveland, Ohio: The Press of Western Reserve University, 1966.

Hocking, W. E. "Marcel and the Ground Issues of Metaphysics." *Philosophy and Phenomenological Research,* Vol. XIV, No. 4 (1954), 439-469.

Keen, Sam. *Gabriel Marcel.* Makers of Contemporary Theology, No. 6. Richmond, Virginia: John Knox Press, 1967.

Luther, Arthur. "Marcel's Metaphysics of the We Are." *Philosophy Today,* Vol. X, No. 314 (1966), 190-203.

McCarty, Donald. "Marcel's Absolute Thou." *Philosophy Today,* Vol. X, No. 314 (1966), 175-181.

Miceli, Vincent P., S. J. *Ascent to Being: Gabriel Marcel's Philosophy of Communion.* New York: Desclée Company, 1965.

O'Malley, John B. *The Fellowship of Being: An Essay on the Concept of Person in the Philosophy of Gabriel Marcel.* The Hague: Martinus Nijhoff, 1966.

Parain-Vial, Jeanne. "The Discovery of the Immediate." *Philosophy Today,* Vol. X, No. 314 (1966), 170-174.

Prini, Pietro. *Gabriel Marcel et la Methodologie de l'Inverifiable.* Paris: Desclée de Brouwer, 1953.

Ricoeur, Paul. *Gabriel Marcel et Karl Jaspers: Philosophie du Mystère et Philosophie du Paradox.* Artistes et Écrivains du Temps Présent. Paris: Éditions du Temps Présent, 1947.

Roberts, David E. *Existentialism and Religious Belief.* Edited by Roger Hazelton. New York: Oxford University Press, 1957.

Schrader, George Alfred, Jr., ed. *Existential Philosophers: Kierkegaard to Merleau-Ponty.* New York: McGraw-Hill, 1967.

Spiegelberg, Herbert. *The Phenomenological Movement: A Historical Introduction.* Phaenomenologica, Nos. 5-6. 2 vols. 2d. ed. The Hague: Martinus Nijhoff, 1969.

Troisfontaines, Roger, S. J. *De l'Existence à Être: La Philosophie de Gabriel Marcel.* Bibliotèque de la Faculté de Philosophie et Lettres de Namur. 2 vols. Louvain: Éditions Nauwelaerts, 1968. Paris: Béatrice-Nauwelaerts, 1968.

_____. *What is Existentialism?* Overview Studies. Albany, New York: Magi Books, Inc., 1968.

Wahl, Jean. *Philosophies of Existence: An Introduction to the Basic Thought of Kierkegaard, Heidegger, Jaspers, Marcel, Sartre.* Translated by F. M. Lory. London: Routledge & Kegan Paul, 1969.

Wild, John. *The Challenge of Existentialism.* Bloomington, Indiana: Indiana University Press, 1955.

Zaner, Richard M. *The Problem of Embodiment: Some Contributions to a Phenomenology of the Body.* Phaenomenologica, No. 17. The Hague: Martinus Nijhoff, 1964

Complementary Works

Berg, J. H. Van Den. "The Human Body and the Significance of Movement." *Philosophy and Phenomenological Research,* Vol. XIII, No. 2 (1952), 159-183.

Bergson, Henri. *The Two Sources of Morality and Religion.* Translated by R. Ashley Audra and Cloudesley Brereton, with the assistance of W. Horsfall Carten. Garden City, New York: Doubleday & Company, Inc., 1935.

Buytendijk, F. J. J. "The Body in Existential Psychology." *Review of Existential Psychology and Philosophy,* Vol. I, No. 2 (1961), 149-172.

Ehman, Robert. "The Phenomenon of World." *Patterns of the Life-World: Essays in Honor of John Wild.* Edited by James Edie, Francis H. Parker and Calvin O. Schrag. Northwestern University Studies in Phenomenology and Existential Philosophy. Evanston: Northwestern University Press, 1970.

Farber, Martin. *Phenomenology and Existence: Toward a Philosophy within Nature.* Harper Torchbooks. New York, Evanston and London: Harper & Row, Publishers, 1967.

Heidegger, Martin. *Being and Time.* Translated by John Macquarrie and Edward Robinson. New York and Evanston: Harper & Row, Publishers, 1962.

Hengstenberg, Hans-Edward. "Phenomenology and Metaphysics of the Human Body." *International Philosophical Quarterly,* Vol. III, No. 2 (1963), 165-200.

Husserl, Edmund. *Cartesian Meditations: An Introduction to Phenomenology.* Translated by Dorian Cairns. The Hague: Martinus Nijhoff, 1960.

_____. *The Crisis of European Sciences and Transcendental Phenomenology.* Translated by David Carr. Northwestern University Studies in Phenomenology and Existential Philosophy. Evanston: Northwestern University Press, 1970.

Jonas, Hans. "Biological Foundations of Individuality." *International Philosophical Quarterly,* Vol. VIII, No. 2 (1968), 231-251.

Landgrebe, Ludwig. "The World as a Phenomenological Problem." *Philosophy and Phenomenological Research,* Vol. I, No. 1 (1940), 38-58.

Merleau-Ponty, Maurice. *Phénoménologie de la Perception.* Bibliotèque des Idees. 10th ed. Paris: Librairie Gallimard.

_____. *Phenomenology of Perception.* Translated by Colin Smith. International Library of Philosophy and Scientific Method. 4th ed. London: Routledge & Kegan Paul, 1967.

_____. *The Primacy of Perception: And Other Essays on Phenomenological Psychology, the Philosophy of Art, History and Politics.* Edited by James M. Edie. Northwestern University Studies in Phenomenology and Existential Philosophy. 2d. ed. Evanston: Northwestern University Press, 1968.

_____. *The Structure of Behavior.* Translated by Alden L. Fisher. 2d. ed. Boston: Beacon Press, 1968.

_____. *The Visible and the Invisible: Followed by Working Notes.* Edited by Claude LeFort. Translated by Alphonso Lingis. Northwestern University Studies in Phenomenology and Existential Philosophy. Evanston: Northwestern University Press, 1968.

Nathanson, Maurice. "The Lebenswelt." *Phenomenology: Pure and Applied.* Edited by Erwin W. Straus. The First Lexington Conference on Pure and Applied Phenomenology. Pittsburgh: Duquesne University Press, 1964.

Ricoeur, Paul. *Fallible Man: Philosophy of the Will.* Translated by Charles Kelbley. 2d. ed. Chicago: Henry Regnery Company, 1967.

_____. *Freedom and Nature: The Voluntary and the Involuntary.* Translated by Erazim V. Kohák. Northwestern University Studies in Phenomenology and Existential Philosophy. Evanston: Northwestern University Press, 1966.

_____. *Philosophie de la Volonté.* Vol. I: *Le Volontaire et l'Involontaire.* Philosophie de l'Esprit. Paris: Éditions Montaigne, 1950.

_____. *The Symbolism of Evil.* Translated by Emerson Buchanan. Religious Perspectives. New York: Harper & Row, Publishers, 1967.

Scheler, Max Ferdinand. *The Nature of Sympathy.* Translated by Peter Heath. London: Routledge & Kegan Paul, 1954.

Schutz, Alfred. *The Phenomenology of the Social World.* Translated by George Walsh and Frederick Lehnert. Northwestern Studies in Phenomenology and Existential Philosophy. Evanston: Northwestern University Press, 1967.

_____. "Some Structures of the Life-World." Collected Papers. Vol. III. *Studies in Phenomenological Philosophy.* Phaenomenologica, No. 22. The Hague: M. Nijhoff, 1970.

Spickler, Stuart F., ed. *The Philosophy of the Body: Rejections of Cartesian Dualism.* Chicago: Quadrangle Books, 1970.

Strasser, Stephan. *The Idea of Dialogal Phenomenology.* Duquesne Studies, Philosophical Series, No. 25. Pittsburgh: Duquesne University Press, 1969.

Wild, John. "Being, Meaning and the World." *Review of Metaphysics,* Vol. XVIII (March, 1965), 411-429.

_____. *Existence and the World of Freedom.* Englewood Cliffs, New Jersey: Prentice-Hall, Inc., 1963.